THE OTHER SIDE

A Journey of Dreams, Delusions and Dilemmas

by

DAVE HOWELL

The Other Side: A Journey of Dreams, Delusions and Dilemmas
ISBN 978-0-9897387-7-4
Copyright © 2020 by David C. Howell

Published by Paladin Publishing
P.O. Box 700515
Tulsa, OK 74170

Text Design/Layout: Lisa Simpson

Printed in the U.S.A.

One of the greatest truths I have learned as a professional counselor is that the person with the greatest courage in the room is the person who allows themselves to be the most vulnerable. At a desperately dark and confusing time in their lives, Dave and Tammye were brave enough to be vulnerable and gave me the privilege of sitting with them as their therapist. I watched as *The Great Counselor* responded to their act of faith, of courage and of vulnerability, and brought them through to *The Other Side* with a stronger, deeper, more intimate, fruitful and authentic relationship than ever before. I cannot wait to see how this exceptional book will help others show similar acts of courage!

—Reverend James W. Grinnell,
Minister at Tulsa Christian Fellowship and
Licensed Marital and Family Therapist at
Crossroads Counseling and Consultation (Tulsa, Oklahoma).
For therapy services, please visit www.crossroadsoftulsa.com

David Howell has always been one of my favorite people and pastors for many reasons. His talent level is off the charts in music, communication and people skills. However, the thing I have enjoyed most about David is his transparency. He is as real and down to earth as they come.

I believe that is why this book is so valuable. There are no pretenses as he charts the journey through difficulty in their relationship and brings you to the other side in victory. Pastors often write in "pious platitudes" and give nice phrases of advice. However, in this book David shares the depths of his aching heart and in a wonderfully refreshing way. The story will give hope to anyone who reads it. It is a great example of the fact that pastors are people too.

—Dr. Bobby Boyles, author and pastor of
Long View Church (Minco, OK)

"Everyone, at some time, has to find *The Other Side*. Dave and Tammye Howell have, but they know that *The Other Side* is an ongoing process of grace that continues in their lives to this day.

Pastors, business leaders, and plain good people, they have been there, done that, and have all of the T-shirts. They have proven themselves, but more than that, they have proven God and the principles of His Word.

I recommend this book to everyone who is looking for *The Other Side*.

—Dr. Leon Stutzman,
founder/pastor Aspire Church and
Science of Empowered Living Fellowship
as well as the author of seven books, including
The Theory of Everything.

"I have had the privilege of getting previews of Pastor Dave's messages before everyone else. During our weekly lunch meetings, he often shared what's in his spirit as it overflowed. I watched many of the chapters of this book unfold in real time, before there was ever a stroke of the keyboard or a mark from a pen. I have watched him walk out *The Other Side* daily.

From my point of view, there is no one more qualified to teach about God's restorative power than Pastor Dave Howell. It is my firm belief that if you will go beyond just reading the personal testimonies and stories revealed in this book, and relate to them, you too will get an understanding of how to get to *The Other Side.*

— Jermaine Mondaine, renowned saxophonist &
national recording artist, associate pastor,
The Bridge at Christ Church; and owner of
Mondaine Media & Marketing Group (Muskogee, OK).

I have known Pastor David Howell for over twenty years. We have worked together as teachers, speakers, musicians, ministers and worship leaders. We have shared many conversations, moments of prayer and also laughs. I can't think of many men today in whom I would entrust my own well-being or that of my family. But this man is one of them.

I admire David's willingness to stand during difficult days, to wait during uncertain times and to trust God when nothing in his circumstances seemed to recommend it. His walk has been inspirational for many of us watching from the bleachers, and I feel confident that anyone who takes the time to get to know him or his wise thoughts will be changed for the better. That's absolutely been true for me.

— Dr. Tim Waters, composer, teacher,
speaker and director of Music Production at
Oral Roberts University.

John 21:25 says, "There are also many other things that Jesus did, which if they were written one by one, I suppose that even the world itself could not contain the books that would be written." That is because Jesus is still writing miracle stories today, and David and Tammye's story is one of those miracle stories. My wife and I have known David and Tammye for 30 years and have walked with them as this miracle story unfolded. It is marvelous in our eyes what the Lord has done! Let their testimony inspire you and lift you to believe that, with God, and our willing cooperation with Him, all things are possible. Believe!

— Jim King, founder of Awaking Hope,
www.awakinghope.com,
and author of *Writings of a Caveman.*

A straightforward and honest look at the challenges of being a pastor, husband and entrepreneur. Pastor Dave lays out the challenges and eventual solutions of what faith in God and trust in His Word can accomplish despite the mountains of adversity one faces on the way to inner peace and the ability to dream again.

—Randy Barr, former pastor, missionary, social worker,
World Bench Press champion and chapel speaker for the
Montreal Expos baseball team

Acknowledgements

The construction of these pages has truly been a lifelong endeavor. The transparency within has been both enlightening and excruciating. I struggled to believe I had the capacity to translate our most delicate moments into a narrative that would inspire and encourage. Yet, deep inside I was confronted with the urgency that someone else needed to hear the anecdotes of faith, failure and family.

I can vividly remember the moment I first heard the challenge within to articulate our story. It was March 5, 2012, our 24th wedding anniversary. We were in the Sheraton Hotel in Puerto Vallarta, Mexico. We were still reeling from our most notable season of impasse.

I began making notes as fast as I could possibly write. That's when I first knew a power greater than I had beckoned me to this cause. Without hesitation, an inner struggle had suddenly turned to a passionate purpose. In less than a moment, the soil had been turned, seeds planted and a harvest of hope began yearning for the light of day. Now more than seven years later, I find myself addressing the final edits.

I can't begin to count the number of times I've encountered a struggling family, a discouraged pastor or a faltering businessman who unintentionally resurrected these pages. Without fail, the discourse of this manuscript erupted in a breath of emotion systematically offering hope to the futility of disappointment. Tears, prayers and compassion seemed to spring forth like a river in a barren desert.

I truly believe this book has the power to transform your life. If you have the courage to receive the seed, the garden will surely grow.

To all those unsuspecting candidates who made an early withdrawal from this manuscript, I am held in your embrace. It was the desperation in your eyes, pleading for help, that continually moved me to finish another page.

To Cynthia Hansen, who was instrumental in speaking into the original rough draft to help get us started in how to position and present this story.

To our congregation, staff, family and friends who persevered through many difficult days, suffering the humiliation and pain of our misgivings, I am forever grateful for your patience and encouragement. Especially to Jerrod and Melissa Adair who routinely reminded me to finish this, and prayed vehemently that inspiration would prevail; you have eternal equity in this harvest.

To my dearest friends, Jermaine and Dee Mondaine, your friendship and support are unequalled. I am overwhelmingly convinced you helped spare my life and save my family. The countless prayers, tears, hugs and rebukes are firmly sewn into the fabric of who I am.

To my parents, Carroll and Betty Howell, the human language is simply not adequate to express my gratitude and appreciation for all you've given me. More than a beating heart, you gave me a firm foundation from which to grow, knowing that in difficult times, a firm footing would prevail. Much like the parable taught by Jesus, you helped me build a house on the Rock rather than sand. The storms did come, and the Rock was enough, unshakable and immovable. Thank you for taking me to church from the moment I was born. For teaching me how to pray, how to dream and how to get back up when I was knocked down. Your love for me goes beyond comprehension, and my heart's embrace for you is greater than words of gratitude could ever portray.

To my gifted son Austin, and his beautiful family, you are the purpose of my life. I will always regret the painful seasons of embarrassment and disappointment you were forced to endure. Though years have separated us in age, your words of wisdom and support have often carried the weight of a seasoned mentor. I truly believe you have the capacity to change the world. Without hesitation, I can boldly say, you have changed mine.

To the queen of our home, the princess of my dreams, my wife, my friend; the captivity of my heart is held in your smile. You've not only been by my side as each chapter was chronicled, you've held my hand as we navigated the uncertain landscapes of life. For thirty plus years we've laughed, loved and lived. This book is not just another story. It's our story. If we had known the perils of our path, we may have chosen a different route. Then again, it is the fragile and colorful steps of our journey that have so gracefully painted our canvas.

For every moment of frustration, we have experienced the reward of perseverance. For every dark and lonely midnight, we have witnessed the restoration of a peaceful sunrise. Pain and disgrace may have presented themselves as the script to our stone; yet determined and resilient ascended to the tribute. Some call it stubborn, while others say persistent. Regardless of the preference, let it forever be published, quitting was never our style.

Thank you for agreeing to walk this road together and allowing me to translate our pain into purpose. Thank you for reminding me day after day that someone needed our story. Thank you for never giving up on us and never giving up on the other side.

I genuinely cherish our Sunday evening drives, where we dream without limits, laugh without reason and love without hesitation. I am eternally grateful for a lifetime of shared memories. Never stop believing in a better life. Never stop caring about others. And whatever you do, never stop singing.

I love you, Tammye Howell. You are without question, the twinkle in my eye.

Foreword

One of the problems that I have always had with "faith books" is that they are not "real world"; that is, they only tell half of the story—the good half. This book is different because Dave and Tammye Howell are different.

I've known the Howell's more years than I want to remember. I was invited to preach a revival by a local pastor. One young man in his late teens stood out. I returned for another meeting the next year and he was still there, and still standing out. I felt a spiritual connection, and during the course of the meeting I was led by the Holy Spirit to confirm the call of God on his life which included speaking a prophetic word over his life. I also gave him a fairly nice, and fairly expensive, diamond ring that had been given to me. The congregation went wild because he was their "fair haired preacher boy." I don't suppose that we exchanged more than a few words, but a God-kind of connection was made. (BTW—I really liked that ring! But, not to worry, the Law of Sowing and Reaping always works, and I've had a lot of much nicer rings since then.)

A few years later Dave made another kind of connection, and married Tammye. Some of the church folk were aghast because Tammye was a lovely young Christian woman but she didn't share Dave's "Holiness" church background, and knowing how these things go, wasn't the one they planned for him. Plus, she was (and is!!) a force in her own right. But it was a good connection and a God connection, and you'll read about it as you go through *The Other Side*.

Did you notice the word "connection" in the last two paragraphs? This book is about connections. Divine connections. Personal connections. Business connections. God-kind of connections. It tells the whole story, the ups and downs, twists and turns, good days, bad days, worse days and better days. It's a "real world book," and as you read it you'll discover an amazing couple who have had an incredible journey. And they're sharing it with you!

A few years later Dave and Tammye invited me to speak at the church that they had begun pastoring in Oklahoma City, Oklahoma. The next year my wife Connie joined me when I returned for a second meeting. The connection became stronger—because that's what connections are supposed to do—become stronger. Over the years I've spoken for the Howell's many times, become privy to their world, seen them experience what you will read about in this book. And I've seen their faith and God's grace as they have met their challenges and prevailed.

Today they pastor a fine church, run several successful companies, as well as a global humanitarian organization. Oh—and that's just a little of what they do.

When Dave first told me that he was writing *The Other Side* I was excited, because I knew that their "real world" experiences would help others to get to *the other side*. It's neither happenstance, nor accident, that has caused you to pick up this book—More than likely it is serendipity, of divine direction that has made that happen. As you read, your faith will grow, solutions will be revealed, and perhaps, I hope, a connection will be made. Because this is a book about connections, and we all need them in our lives. I'm thankful for the connection . . . I've counted it up . . . over forty years . . . that we have had with Dave and Tammye Howell.

You'll be thankful that you've read this book.

Happy Reading,

Dr. Leon Stutzman

Founder and pastor of Aspire Church (Dayton, OH)
and Science of Empowered Living Fellowship.
He is also the author of seven books,
including *The Theory of Everything*.

Table of Contents

Introduction

In the summer of 2009, my family and I were facing the most difficult challenge we had ever faced. Tattered and torn, we were barely able to function. It seemed that a lifetime of winning and a legacy of stability had finally reached its breaking point. Everything that mattered was weighing in the balance. It seemed every breath would be our last.

Friends and supporters that once held to every word we spoke were nowhere to be found, like sailors jumping from a sinking ship. Then again, who could blame them? Our ship was sinking, and sinking fast it was. Most were amazed that we were still afloat. Somehow and for some reason known only to God, we were still alive.

Every day, we expected the next wave of disaster to sweep over the bough and finish off the nightmare we couldn't seem to rise from. Beat up, bruised and battered by the worst storm we had ever faced, we were ready to give up and let life, or death, claim the last fragment of hope.

As the grim reaper of devastation and destruction hovered over what was left of our weary souls, we felt compelled to do something drastic and completely uncharacteristic of someone in our plight. We bought two tickets and boarded a plane. We flew halfway across the country to an end we couldn't predict.

It was the fourth of July, a day celebrating freedom. It was a parody of uncharted chasms. The endless depth of hopelessness that bled through our red, white and blue celebration was awkward at best. A toast for freedom seemed highly insensitive for two who were bound with such despair.

**It was then, we first heard the words that
would forever correct our compass.**

Profoundly clear and with unparalleled precision, the words were deposited into our innermost being. It felt like a warm healing balm being poured over us. Still distraught and weary, yet something or someone was breathing hope back into us.

We couldn't begin to imagine how nor how long it would take; but we believed these words were a lighthouse in the distance, guiding us to safety. It was perhaps the very reason for this trip. We had flown far enough away from the darkness that we were finally able to glimpse a sliver of light penetrating the dense fog.

To this day, we are ever grateful for those gentle, yet overtly powerful words. The calming voice of comfort and peace speaking life into our souls. The words that would become the prevailing wind in our sails . . . *the other side*.

An Important Word to the Reader

As we retrace our perilous journey of dreams, delusions and dilemmas, I hope that our trek will enlighten, inspire and challenge you to navigate your own path to freedom and peace.

This book is for every person who has faced a problem beyond their scope of understanding. For the pastor who resigns every Sunday afternoon in frustration, only to pick up the mantle again on Monday. For the marriage that has failed beyond the advice of counselors. For the businessman teetering on bankruptcy. For the addict relentlessly pleading for one more chance to be clean.

After thirty-plus years of full-time pastoral ministry and leading various businesses, I am keenly aware that problems knock on the door of every race, every color, every degree of education and every social status. I have witnessed the tragic and the triumphant, the impossible and the unbelievable. Yet, one thing is constant: anything is possible if you believe.

A dear friend once enlightened me with a simple and profoundly deep insight. "As long as there are people, they will do what people do."

For various reasons, I have never forgotten this statement. Why did they do that? How did they get there? What will they do now? It's just possible, if you're reading this book, you've replaced "they" with your own reflection.

Smart people do dumb things. People in love commit horrific acts of betrayal, often against the ones they love the most. Spiritual giants trade in a keen sense of divine insight for a doctorate from Satanic U.

It doesn't make sense. It doesn't seem possible, but it happens every day. You can trace it all the way back to Adam and Eve who talked face-to-face with God; and still, they succumbed to the enemy's seduction. Judas and Peter walked hand in hand with Jesus, and they too found opportunity to express the fallibility of their humanity. If there's breath in your body, you're a candidate for both success and failure.

Don't think for a minute that problems and betrayals are exclusive to the evil and devious. Trouble has no preference in choosing its next victim. Its only purpose is to disrupt and destroy the lives of healthy and happy people.

This book may not solve your problems, but it is sure to give you hope that a solution is possible. As you engage in our life's stories, find the reflection of yours. From stories of childhood friends and lifelong dreams, remember where you've been and who has been there with you. Remember how you felt when trouble came, how it affected you, how it changed you.

You are certain to find nuggets of truth embedded in these stories of humor, tragedy and perseverance. This book is not a tell-all for every dark secret of our lives. It is neither an embellishment of the facts nor a glorification of the failures. While many of our most embarrassing and frustrating seasons are outlined in these pages, other elements must remain covered by the blood of Christ.

This book is an account of the various scenarios that brought us to our knees. It is also a compilation of revelations, processes and techniques that helped us overcome incredible challenges and rise to a new level of existence.

The other side is not about quitters. It's about relentless tenacity to survive and thrive. It's not about our weaknesses, but rather our courageous drive to never give up on our dreams.

It is our prayer that this book become a window into the eternal soul called "you." It is entirely possible that you too are facing paramount challenges that have brought you to your proverbial knees. The names and dates may look different, but it is the same evil conspirator who has targeted you.

The other side of your peril may look completely different than ours. Nonetheless, if you're willing to explore the possibility of a fresh start and a better life, then continue reading. I'm confident you'll find yourself somewhere within these pages.

One morning, not so far away, you'll wake up and realize you're no longer trapped in a nightmare. You've arrived at a place you barely dreamed existed, but exist it does and you're there . . . *The Other Side*.

Chapter 1

The Dreamer

The short version may read something like this: Boy meets girl. Boy likes girl. Boy and girl live happily ever after. Unfortunately, the short version has a few holes in it. The long version would most definitely not fit on these pages, so I'll try to find a happy medium.

It's important to understand where we came from. This may not completely reveal how we got to where we are, but it will most certainly shed light on where we want to go, or in some cases, where we don't.

Do you remember how you started? Where you came from? How you met the love of your life? What you talked about in those days? Where you spent your money, if you had any? Do you remember the dreams and aspirations of your youth? All those great plans and schemes that would make you excessively rich before your twenty-ninth birthday? The person you wanted to fall in love with, have a house full of kids and spend the rest of your life with?

It seems like two lifetimes ago. The dreams, the hopes and the *"someday I'm gonna's"* consumed my every thought. I was full of those dreams. I felt like Joseph in the Bible. They called him the dreamer. That was me. I was a dreamer.

I can remember being that little boy, so full of grand ideas and an overwhelming sense of purpose. Deep inside, I knew I was placed on this earth to do something great. I knew I had destiny living in me. Purpose would be my playground and success was just another way to spell my name. Confidence was not something I lacked.

My father had taught me to play the guitar and sing before I even started to school. At twelve, my mother volunteered me to teach the four- and five-year-old boys' Sunday school class. As a teenager, I directed the Wednesday evening children's ministry at our church. I became a licensed minister at age seventeen, before I graduated from high school. Immediately after graduation, I was off to Bible college and to change the world.

There was no question about where I was going in life and what I would do. I had a gift and a calling. I would preach and sing my way across the country and someday around the world. One thing was certain, I knew what my legacy would look like. I hadn't lived it yet, but in my mind, I had already been there.

There was just one critical piece to my dream that I needed to figure out. Who would go with me on this sensational journey? Who would be willing to give up their dreams in order to embrace mine; or better yet, another dreamer with whom I could dream? Who would want to spend the rest of their life solving problems and helping others find peace, purpose and comfort? In my mind, I was thinking who wouldn't?

It was December 20th, 1985. I was scheduled to sing for a friend's wedding. The song was one of the most popular graduation and wedding songs of the 80's. *"We've Only Just Begun."*[1]

How fitting this would be the song, because it truly was where *"we"* began.

A girl I worked with was playing the piano for the wedding, and she played while I sang. We knew each other socially, but not much. We worked together at a clothing store, and this was about the depth of our friendship. We had very little in common. Our friends were different. Even our preference of music was different. I was a suave, dapper, extremely cool, soon to be millionaire. (Okay, truthfully I was a nerd with no money; but I had dreams.)

She was tall and thin, dressed in the latest fashion and popular with all the cool people. She must have been an angel that had fallen from heaven. (And no . . . I didn't use that line on her. I did write her a song called *"My Angel Love,"* but I saved it for a really special moment later on.) I had never noticed her before. I had noticed her distinctly red hair and that she looked like a model out of a magazine. To be completely honest, she was way out of my league.

I didn't know she played the piano, but play she did. In those days, everyone knew that a preacher's wife had to play the piano. This is interesting, I thought. Can she sing? I wondered. I would later find out that she really "likes to sing." This girl is not just cool and pretty, she's actually a smokin' hot babe who plays the piano and "likes to sing."

After the wedding rehearsal, we decided to go for a snack at a local pizza joint. I'll never forget that night. We sat at a little table for two, next to the window. Two things stood out to me that night: it was snowing outside, and this girl was the prettiest girl in the whole wide world.

How was it that we had been working together, only a few feet apart, yet never had a meaningful conversation? That was about to change. Every night for the next six or seven weeks, we talked. We talked about everything imaginable. Politics, religion, music, how cool I was, etc., etc.

Who was this girl? Where did she come from? What does she like? Who does she like?

The next day, after that wedding rehearsal, I went back to work and told my friend, "I'm gonna marry that girl someday." He laughed.

In the spring of 1988, I did just what I said. I married that girl. At our wedding, I sang the song I had written for her. My dreams were coming true. Now, there were two dreamers. Heaven had smiled on us. We were meant for each other. Surely no other couple on the entire planet could be so perfect for each other. At last, that missing piece of my puzzle was in place. The only thing left was for us to live out the dream.

We were headed for a very special place filled with blissful tranquility. Unfortunately, our yellow brick road would have some major potholes along the way.

Chapter 2

Two Old Goats

The world as we knew it would soon be different. Our journey together was underway, and nothing could stop us from living out our fairy tale. Perhaps, if we hadn't been so blinded by the bright lights just ahead of us, we may have noticed some very important cracks in our armor.

It was the night before the big day. It was our wedding rehearsal. The time when everything is supposed to be perfect. It wasn't.

Suddenly, the universe was becoming clear. This angel had apparently been one of the angels kicked out of heaven with Satan. Of course, I was now viewed as Satan's spawn, and our dream was showing inclinations of a nightmare.

We had thought we were nothing alike. Actually, we were absolutely alike in so many ways. A staggering truth was being revealed. We're not prized thoroughbred race horses at all. We're two mules staring eyeball to eyeball, arguing over what shade of blue the sky is.

It was the worst fight we had ever had, to this point. It seems so petty now. Ridiculous and extremely childish.

My soon to be brother-in-law was video-taping our rehearsal and would handle the same responsibility in the wedding. The "discussion" was over the lights. Should the lights be on or off? Dim or bright? How dim? If they're too dim, the camera won't be able to capture a clear picture. If they're too bright, the whole intimate effect of this very special moment would be lost.

The fury of hell was about to be released, and we were the ones opening the gates.

"You can't talk to me that way! What's wrong with you? Stop being so difficult! You're acting like a child! Let me handle this! I know what I'm doing and you don't!" These were certainly not the wedding vows we had previously discussed.

What was happening? Two dreamers in love are not supposed to act this way. The world is supposed to be fluffy and happy with fairy dust falling from the sky.

It is sad and often repulsive how we allow such small, insignificant matters to completely disrupt the most important moments of our lives.

> ❧
>
> *It is sad and often repulsive how we allow such small, insignificant matters to completely disrupt the most important moments of our lives.*

The brother-in-law's ability to film the ceremony was not the issue. The lights were not the issue. We were the issue!

We were both young, full of ambition and absolutely convinced that we were right about anything and everything. We had somehow lost the essence of the moment, along with the purpose of our union. How could we ever change the world if we weren't first willing to change ourselves?

Dreams often face delusions and dilemmas. It's not a matter of *"if,"* but *"when."* You *will* have challenges. You *will* face trials. You *will* have moments when you do or say something that you regret for many years to come. To this day, I am disappointed in the way we acted at our wedding rehearsal.

We forever squandered an opportunity for one of the most meaningful moments in our life. Perplexingly so, we can never recapture the innocence lost on that special night.

Selfishness has no place in your dreams. The moment you become selfish, you lose the power that propels you to your purpose. Jesus recognized this truth. He said, in John 5:30, *". . .for I seek not to please myself. . . ."* [2]

I am firmly convinced that 99 percent of all marital issues are caused by selfishness. The other 1 percent can be attributed to those who only want their way. It is imperative that our dreams and aspirations are grounded solidly on the premise that life is not about us.

I have witnessed individuals who adamantly and vehemently insisted that any connotations or references to submission and obedience be removed from their wedding vows. This is directly and blatantly in opposition to the core meaning of love. How can you truly love unless you are willing to lay aside your wants and offer yourself as a servant to the needs of the one to whom you pledge?

First Corinthians 13:5, in its classical and biblical definition of *"love"* says,

"It is not self-seeking and it does not demand its own way" (NIV/NLT).

> *I am firmly convinced that 99 percent of all marital issues are caused by selfishness.*

I remember hearing my pastor tell a story about two mountain goats. They were high up in the mountains on a steep grade, and the trail they travelled was extremely narrow.

The problem wasn't their inability to walk on this narrow and difficult path. They were both well capable of navigating this course with great precision. The problem was that they were heading straight toward each other and would soon be face to face. Since the trail was only wide enough for one, there was no way for them to pass beside each other. If they tried, one of them would surely plummet to an untimely demise.

Would it be a battle of strength and will? Would they oppose each other on this trail and launch themselves headlong into a struggle for supremacy? Would they fight for preeminence and the right to continue traveling their personal course? Which one is stronger? Which one is the bravest warrior? Which one is more determined?

It would be easy to draw parallels to the conflicts we face on a daily basis. Whether at work, school or church, but especially marriage. All too often our dilemmas have simple solutions that are clouded by our insensitive, arrogant, need-to-be-right attitudes of selfishness and greed.

The best solution to your dilemma may be somewhat different than you had originally considered.

Something fascinating and completely uncharacteristic happened on that narrow mountain trail. As they approached the moment of truth, the do or die, the fight of a lifetime, the right to stand tall as the champion of champions, something no one expected to see took place. Suddenly, it was not about who was stronger, more powerful or more determined.

———

One goat simply bowed himself gently to his knees, while the other leaped effortlessly right over the top, and both continued on their journey. Such wisdom. Such intuitiveness and creativity. Such grace. Such humility from two otherwise proud beings.

Is it possible that two hard-headed mountain goats have a greater understanding of unified purpose than we? Neither had to die. Neither had to fight. It may be part of their nature and personality to butt heads, but it was not their inclination to die in futility over a problem that was not a problem at all.

One of my dearest mentors would often say, "Don't throw away the baby with the dirty bathwater." You may find yourself in a quandary from time to time, but don't launch yourself into the oblivion of peril, simply because you're uncomfortable or can't seem to find a clear solution.

> *Is it possible that two hard-headed mountain goats have a greater understanding of unified purpose than we?*

The value of your dreams, friends and especially your family are far too great to throw away every time you have a bad day. Problems are a matter of perspective. A spilled glass of milk is life-altering to a three-year-old. It should not be the same catastrophe for a person of thirty.

Hopefully, our journey will yield nuggets of wisdom along the way. With the correct solution, a problem that once stopped the world from turning could easily be a bump in the road or a casual passing of two goats on a mountain trail.

For these old goats on a mountain trail, *the other side* was achievable without a struggle. As you navigate your journey, allow the collective wisdom of your past to assist you. Don't allow the enemy

Don't allow the enemy to bait you into conflict when you have the wisdom to avoid it.

to bait you into conflict when you have the wisdom to avoid it.

Thankfully, we were able to navigate past that ridiculously childish argument at our wedding rehearsal. We would soon encounter more obstacles and challenges. The question remained, would we learn how to deal with adversity properly or hold on to our present identity which was often more stubborn than a couple of old goats?

Chapter 3

I Cross My Heart

Moving forward in harmony was definitely a priority for us. We quickly recognized the need to set aside our differences and unite our souls. We were committed to living out our matrimonial vows one day at a time. If we were going to spend a lifetime together, we needed it to be in unity.

We finally agreed, I was right and she was wrong. (I'm only joking.) Indeed, we had a beautiful wedding and yes, the video turned out fine.

We were gaining a priceless revelation of how to resolve conflict. This powerful process would prove invaluable later on in life.

We were just kids trying to find our way. We recognized there was something different about us. Pursuing our destiny and changing the world was definitely on our minds, but first we had a little homework to do.

Though the wedding rehearsal was our most significant argument to this point, it was certainly not our first dilemma. Many of the deep conversations we had while dating were about our religious beliefs.

Tammye came from a Southern Baptist background whereas I came from a Pentecostal Holiness background. The doctrinal differences of our upbringing are not important to this story. What is of importance is the conflict caused by our differences.

For those who argue that religion is not important in a relationship, I would argue they have not explored the depths of faith and family. As we hold our faith close to our heart, we also hold dear the practices and ordinances that accompany it.

Differences in faith have caused nations to go to war. Obviously, these same differences can cause families to face conflict. Our differences were such that we both knew our relationship would struggle unless we found resolution.

> ❧
>
> *For those who argue that religion is not important in a relationship, I would argue they have not explored the depths of faith and family.*

I was a licensed minister, preparing for a career in the ministry; thus my wife and I would need to be in agreement for the doctrine we would share.

Rather than argue, we thought it best to go on a spiritual quest for the personal revelation we would need to embrace as husband and wife. This is much easier said than done.

For me, the all-knowing one (or maybe I was the know it all), I had commonly accepted that I knew what I believed. Unfortunately, I had missed the "why." Our spiritual quest had put me in unfamiliar territory. Suddenly, I was not only trying to reassure Tammye, but also myself of what I believed and why.

As I searched for answers to secure my position, Tammye did the same. She wrote down a series of questions and made an appointment to visit with her pastor.

To this day, I appreciate his candor and demeanor in how he answered. He openly stated that regardless of how he personally felt about certain scriptures, he was bound by the organization in which he served to teach a particular point of view. He went on to say, it would be well worth the time for Tammye to search out her own view of these passages and come to a clear conviction on her own.

As harmless as this all sounds, pressure was mounting on both sides of the aisle for us to arrive at a common conviction. When I say "pressure," I mean our families and friends were strongly encouraging us to make decisions that were beyond our level of comfort.

I've visited with many families over the years who have faced immense challenges due to a difference of beliefs. Some will quote Bible verses about "being unequally yoked together." Though there is scripture that teaches along this line, it is talking about believers being married to unbelievers.

The Apostle Paul gave great caution to the dangers associated with this area. Likewise, he gave ample instruction about how to handle such a situation should it arise.

Scripture inclines that believers are not recognized by their differences but by their likeness. That common ground being a belief that Jesus Christ is the Son of God who gave His life in crucifixion for the sins of mankind, then rose from the grave to consummate a new covenant. God does not label us as Jew or Greek, Baptist or Presbyterian, Pentecostal or Lutheran, black or white, Republican or Democrat.

These labels come from man, not from God. It would be helpful for all of us to remove the labels and simply come together. It's been noted, when we get to heaven, we will only be known as His children.

I was working at my home church, which was a radical Pentecostal group. Loud, live music. Fiery preaching. Speaking in tongues. Prayer lines, complete with laying on of hands and lots of anointing oil. Tammye played the piano for a healthy and thriving Southern Baptist church, which was much more reserved in its presentation of the Gospel. Both churches were sound and both groups proclaimed a definitive love for God.

> ✄
> *It would be helpful for all of us to remove the labels and simply come together.*

As our relationship continued to grow and the dilemma of religion continued to hover, we knew a decision had to be made before we could move forward.

Other people, some who were family members, had taken it upon themselves to push us in a particular direction and help us make a decision that aligned with their personal convictions. Snide comments were being made. We were being shunned at social gatherings. Rumors and lies were being passed around about our relationship. All the while, tension over our religious preferences continued to grow.

It's worth mentioning that not all conflict is self-induced. Some issues are created by others and some are just natural by-products of putting two imperfect people together and asking them to become one.

I've often used the analogy of being involved in a bank robbery. For instance, suppose you were in the bank, simply conducting routine business when the bad guys come in to rob it. In the confusion and a subsequent altercation, you and the bad guy are both injured. You did nothing wrong, yet you've been injured by someone else's actions.

This is true in all aspects of life. Other people's problems can have a negative effect on us. Their discontent causes us frustration. Their indiscretion puts us in a challenging place. Their mismanagement causes hardships we would not have experienced otherwise.

Prayerfully, Tammye and I came to a decision that we would embrace our faith in a Pentecostal manner. Above and beyond all the challenges, we felt as though God had embraced us with a unique and special grace that helped us find this path.

As far as those who were causing problems for us, we decided to love them unconditionally. Regardless of how they had treated us or what they may have said about us, we were going to love them. It's interesting to note, over the next few months, several of those individuals found themselves facing life-threatening challenges.

Each time they found themselves in dire straits, we made our way to them and offered prayers and support to help them overcome their dilemma. One by one, they all came through and survived their battles.

In the end, they had not only survived their challenges, but now they were some of our strongest supporters. Their disapproval of our decisions on faith had become irrelevant. They now recognized us for the unity we shared, as well as the faith we carried close to our hearts.

In your path to the other side, you will certainly encounter others who will cause great pain and discomfort for you. My advice is to love them unconditionally and pray for them daily. It's not your responsibility to change everyone else. Nor is it your responsibility to convince them of who's right and who's wrong.

> *In your path to the other side, you will certainly encounter others who will cause great pain and discomfort for you. My advice is to love them unconditionally and pray for them daily.*

They may get under your skin. They may irritate you like a bad rash. They may say all manner of terrible things about you. No matter, hold true to your course. Let faith be your guide. Whatever you do, don't get bitter. One of my mentors would often say, "If you don't get bitter, you'll make it."

Today, Tammye's and my faith are stronger than ever. It was important for us to iron out the wrinkles early in our relationship so that later on we were able to fall back on the revelations we uncovered in those early days.

> ❧
> *Establishing a certainty of what you believe and why will most assuredly help keep you on the right path.*

As we faced problems that were incrementally more difficult, we were able to use the same methods to find the appropriate answers for each situation.

Trust me when I say, as you set your compass toward the other side, your belief system will be challenged like never before. Having established a certainty of what you believe and why will most assuredly help keep you on the right path.

Chapter 4

Climbing the Ladder

As Tammye and I navigate our path to *the other side*, it's important to understand some of the success we have enjoyed along the way. There were seasons when it seemed everything we touched turned to gold. Times when everything seemed to work out in a perfect way, regardless of how many stupid mistakes we made. I'm convinced there was a special grace being poured over us. I've often said, "Much of our success was in spite of what we did, not because."

January of 1990 would find us transitioning away from a very successful season as youth pastors in our hometown.

We moved a short two hours away to Oklahoma City where we would take a more responsible role as senior pastors of a small church. The little church had been through a tumultuous time and was struggling to find direction. Our arrival seemed to bring a breath of freshness to the congregation. I'm not implying we were anything special. Simply stated, the dreams and visions in our heart were aligned almost perfectly with the vision of this small group.

It was like God Himself had destined our paths to cross. In fact, two years previous to our arrival, a dear friend of mine had gone to preach at this little church. At the same time, I felt a divine leading on the inside say to me, "Someday you are going to that church."

And now, two years later, there we were. It was Saturday night. We had met up with the head deacon and his wife for dinner. Later that evening, they drove us to see the church.

We were just ten feet inside the doors of the church when it hit us. Tammye and I both began to cry. We looked at each other as if the entire universe had taken time out of its busy schedule to say, "This is your new home."

I can't begin to tell you how special that season was. The eternal impact that season had on our lives was divinely orchestrated. For nearly eight years, we found success after success in that place. Sure, we had our share of challenges, and some of them were significant; but over all, it was one of the most beautiful seasons of our young lives.

We made friends who became family. We encountered victories that could not be explained in the natural. We witnessed the hand of an Almighty God bless us far beyond anything we could ever have deserved. Yet, in the midst of it all, we were just kids learning about life.

> *As much as we would like to take credit for everything that goes right in our lives, we must understand that our success is directly tied to those around us.*

Many times I have wished that I could go back to that special season. Without question, I would have done some things differently. First, I would have been more humble about the success we enjoyed. Second, I would have taken more time to appreciate the season.

As much as we would like to take credit for everything that goes right in our lives, we must understand that our success is directly tied to those around us. We are a team. In this case, we were a family. It's been said many times, "No man is an island." This truth is well worth remembering, especially when everything is going well.

Never get so busy climbing the ladder of success that you forget to appreciate those who are supporting your climb. You may need those same people to help cushion your fall.

Indeed, there were times when we needed someone to help cushion our fall. I am forever grateful for the friends who have stood by our side regardless of the season.

Today, when the schedule is heavy and so many things are pulling me in different directions, I remember the lessons I learned in that Oklahoma City season in our lives, particularly when it comes to time management.

I've learned the phone will ring again tomorrow. There will always be another time to read emails or check in on social media. There will always be another meeting, another business lunch, another attempt to hijack my time. These *"time bandits"* will always be around.

> *It's up to me to determine which items are worthy of my time.*

The Apostle Paul used an appropriate expression when he challenged us to *"redeem the time."*[3] That's exactly what I try to remember now. My time is important, and it's up to me to determine which items are worthy of that time.

You see, some day I will look back on this current season and most likely wish I had done some things differently. So why not make those assessments now? Why not spend more time with my family? Why not enjoy those special moments with my wife?

Why not leave the office early and go fishing with my father or cancel lunch with a new client so I can take my mother to lunch at her favorite restaurant? Why not interrupt that important phone call because my son just walked in the office and wants to visit?

Why not have someone else preach next Sunday, while my wife and I go out of town for no particular reason? Why not . . . ?

If you're anything like I WAS, you too may find it difficult to say "no" to those embezzling thieves of time.

STOP!!! RIGHT NOW, STOP WHATEVER YOU'RE DOING!

Take a deep breath and ask yourself, "What is the most important thing that I could be doing at this very moment? What is it that I need to do today, that I may not be able to do tomorrow?"

Today, I live my life differently, and for good reasons. I have different priorities than most. I have a different perspective than most. I have a different opinion of where I need to be and what I need to be giving my time and attention to.

> *Living today with peace of mind is better than living tomorrow with sorrow and regrets.*

If you had been where I've been and faced the challenges that I've faced, you too may find a difference in your choices.

Living today with peace of mind is better than living tomorrow with sorrow and regrets.

One of my mentors in business offered some critical advice back when Tammye and I were newlyweds. He was a very successful man with a large business.

He explained to me how he had a gift for business. He understood how to make money, and he made a lot of it. He went on to also explain that he wasn't very good at taking time off away from the business, and sharing that time with his family.

He encouraged me to take time away from my busy schedule and spend quality time with my family. He added, "Take a vacation every year. Even if you have to borrow the money, take a vacation. You can pay the money back later. After all, a few days of quality time with your family is far less costly than counseling or divorce."

I found his advice to be very profitable. Oh, the times that I've remembered his words. Times when our schedule was so crazy, I remembered what he had spoken to me. I always did my best to heed that advice. In fact, every year since we've been married, we've taken a family vacation. And yes, there have been a few times that I had to borrow the money and once we even had to borrow a vehicle.

People who are driven to succeed often find it difficult to lay aside the "routine" and give themselves a break. I have talked with people who have massive amounts of vacation built up, but refuse to take any time off. They're convinced the company just can't make it without them. Let me help you with something.

THE WORK WILL STILL BE THERE WHEN YOU COME BACK!

Pastors are often the worst offenders in this group. We typically feel pressure from members of the congregation or influential people who make us feel like it's some kind of horrid sin for the pastor to be gone on a Sunday. Yet, these same manipulators have no remorse when they skip church for three months every summer. I realize there is a tremendous responsibility on pastors. However, there is a higher responsibility on husbands and fathers. We never want our family to feel as if we value our career above them, even if our chosen profession is pastoring.

> *THE WORK WILL STILL BE THERE WHEN YOU COME BACK!*

I recently overheard a lady talking about taking a vacation with her husband. I couldn't believe what I was hearing. She said they had not been on a vacation in over ten years. That's absurd.

I've heard people say how they feel guilty for taking time off. Why would you feel guilty? You need that time off. You need a break from the daily grind. You need to get away from the business of your life and let yourself unwind for a few days. You owe it to yourself. More importantly, you owe it to your family.

Even God rested on the seventh day. Jesus routinely pulled away from the crowds to find a place to rest. If you think you're holding the high ground by working all those hours, think again.

> *If you think you're holding the high ground by working all those hours, think again.*

Find a peaceful place to enjoy the sunset and just hold hands with the one you love. Tell them how important they are to you. Do your best to convince them that they are many times over more important than your career, your ministry, your friends, your hobbies or anything else that might find its way into your busy schedule.

Show your family how valuable they are to you. They will see the depth of your commitment. Not because you spend money on them, but rather because you spend time with them.

Once again, a little quiet time and a few days off might do more good than you imagine. It is one of the keys to help you reach *the other side*.

Starting out, I thought we were being very diligent about managing our time. Every year we took a vacation. Every Monday we closed the office and we had family time. Still to this day, I am rarely in the office on Monday. That time is set aside for my family and me.

I look at it this way. The first day of the week, Sunday, belongs to God, primarily because He is my highest priority. The second day, Monday, belongs to my wife and family. Then everyone else can get in line and make an appointment for whatever time is left. I'm happy to accommodate as many as possible, but it's my life and I get to decide where I spend my time.

This has been my modus operandi for more than thirty years now. I realize your schedule may be a bit different than mine; however, I hope you can see my reasoning. You have to make time for your family, or the time may come when you don't have a family to make time for.

As hard as I tried to keep those *"time bandits"* out of my daily planner, they always seemed to find a sneaky and untimely moment to crash the party.

As a pastor, I wanted to do everything I could to serve the needs of our congregation. As a very young pastor, I wasn't always afforded the freedom to rearrange my schedule in order to fit the needs of my family.

There's always a meeting to attend. Always some kind of support group getting together. Always a music rehearsal to get ready for the big day, and every Sunday's a big day.

> *You have to make time for your family, or the time may come when you don't have a family to make time for.*

There is always someone in the hospital who needs prayer. Always a family in crisis who needs counseling. Always an important phone call. Always a phone call that someone else thought was important. Did I mention the phone calls?

As we strive to achieve success and ascend the ranks of public approval, we often have difficulty prioritizing essential vs. nonessential matters. You may have a gift at balancing a budget, but your family deserves more than a healthy bottom line.

As our ministry began to grow, so did the restraints on my time. Every day and every night was calling for a piece of my life. Looking back, this is where I should've made serious adjustments. I'm not trying to lay the blame on anyone else; not the church, not business, not my desire to succeed and certainly not on my family. I take full responsibility for my decisions. To regret or rejoice, I have to own the moment.

Looking back, I believe the increasing demands for my time was most likely a key area that first began to cause serious cracks in the foundation of our family.

I was a committed husband and father. We took those vacations every year. Monday was our family day. We did a lot of things right. As far as anyone could tell, we were the perfect little family. Everything was as good as it could get. We were well on our way to the top.

You see, it isn't that you had to take ONE important call during dinner. It isn't that you had to work late ONCE or that you had to send ONE more email before going to bed. It isn't the ONE time that hurts. It's when ONE time starts happening every day.

Before you know it, you're working late three or four nights every week. You're gone with your friends on Saturday. You're helping with the Christmas program at school. You're coaching a Little League team with your neighbor. The phone is either glued to your ear or you're constantly texting someone about all the *"important"* stuff that needs to get done tomorrow. You may not realize it's happening, but I promise your family sees it.

Don't let your drive to succeed impede your path to happiness.

Many believe that working harder or longer will yield greater success. As much as I believe in working hard and completing the task at hand, I also believe there must be a vigilant cognizance of the ante.

As a young man, I encountered an expression from a book by the same name, *Work Smarter Not Harder.*[4]

> *Don't let your drive to succeed impede your path to happiness.*

I tried hard to employ this strategy. Unfortunately, this mind-set was rarely encouraged by my closest mentors. Thus, I often found myself working harder and longer days hoping to at least gain the approval of both my shepherds and my flock. Sadly, the success I gained was countered by a weakened marriage.

There are thousands of career opportunities and millions of chances to prove your worth to the world, but only one family you can call your own.

Your journey to *the other side* will be much sweeter if your family is there to enjoy it with you.

Chapter 5

The Little Dreamer

It seemed like the perfect time. Everything was going great. Our son was born. The church was growing. We were opening a new facility. Business was up. Life was good.

It's hard to imagine how everything can go so right and so wrong—all at the same time.

The birth of our only child, Austin, is definitely one of the greatest pleasures of my life. To say that I am extremely proud of him, would be a gross understatement of the truth. He is more than I could have asked for in a son. He is smart, talented, gifted and anointed. Now an adult, he is a great husband and father. He's a great friend. Not to be overlooked, he possesses a true world-changer mind-set. He is a dreamer, much like his dad.

> *It's hard to imagine how everything can go so right and so wrong—all at the same time.*

His arrival, though blessed and special, was not without difficulty. For reasons unknown, he decided to be born some seven weeks early.

Because of his early arrival, his little body had not fully developed. The doctors immediately placed him in the Neonatal Intensive Care

Unit (NICU), complete with a horrid nest of wires and tubes, encasing him inside a small glass box. Though appropriately designed to keep him safe from the outside world, it seemed more like a sarcophagus for a priceless treasure.

It was unbearable to see our greatest promise in this place of apparent defeat.

Tammye was not allowed to even hold him at the moment of birth. She was told that he was weak and needed immediate medical attention. Prayers were definitely in order.

Over the next few days, the doctors informed us that Austin would never be normal and that his lungs would never fully develop. They believed he would be a runt, with obvious abnormalities and would not be able to run and play like other kids. They declared he would never enjoy the pleasures of a normal body and certainly not the experience of a normal childhood *"that is . . . if he even makes it."*

Our hearts were broken at a time we had patiently waited for with great expectations. We quickly learned how painful it is to see your child in a place of need. We cried. We cried. Then, we cried some more.

> *A demonic strategy was not only aimed at Austin's tiny little body, it was a direct attack on his destiny.*

This perfect little boy was being attacked before he ever had a chance to crawl across the floor. A demonic strategy was not only aimed at Austin's tiny little body, it was a direct attack on his destiny.

Storm clouds had begun to gather over our beautiful sea of tranquility.

Austin was born on Sunday morning. It was now Wednesday night, and there was no apparent change in his condition. He was alive, but struggling. The doctors informed us that Tammye would be discharged from the hospital. We were also apprized that Austin would need an extended stay in the NICU. It was unbearable to hear we would have to go home without our beautiful promise.

Unable to hold him and caress his frail little body, we hovered over his glass box and tearfully tried to explain why we were leaving the hospital without him. The words on this page are not descriptive enough to express our pain and sense of hopelessness.

Another young couple in the church came to the hospital to help us gather our things. To this day, I remember their words of encouragement and support. They refused to let us focus on the pain. Rather, they challenged us to live through the life-giving faith we shared with them every Sunday. Their words would prove more valuable than they could ever know.

As we departed, the doctors explained that Austin would need to stay in the hospital for an undetermined length of time, possibly months. They were, however; cautiously optimistic that he would live. Even so, it was clear that Austin would likely face the aforementioned challenges; inasmuch, he would need to be under constant medical attention.

I still remember the emptiness of walking into our house that night, especially our baby's room. The decor was spectacular. It had been ready for weeks. Bright colors. A custom mural on the wall. Every detail touched by the hands of a new mother, ready for the grand voyage that awaits.

Sadly, the soft and fluffy teddy bear was missing the company of his destiny as he lay alone on an empty pillow.

Before going to bed that night, we knelt on the floor beside an empty crib. We reminded God that Austin was our promise and a blessing from heaven. We declared, by faith, that he would not be weak and sickly like the doctors had proposed. We proclaimed that our little promise would be strong and healthy—a vibrant life, full of strength. We refused to accept anything less.

With heavy hearts and eyes swollen from crying, we laid our heads on the pillow, held hands and prayed for a miracle. I vividly recall the despair that seemed to wake us every time we found the courage to fall asleep. Through the night, I did my best to hold Tammye close. It was anything but easy. Several times we discussed driving back to the hospital, some thirty minutes away, just to peek in on our promise.

We knew this was nothing more than a sinister attack from the enemy. More times than I can count, we walked a lonely floor that night through the house, down the hall and into Austin's empty room. Broken and shattered, we tearfully prayed, "Father God, please help us. Give us peace, and touch Austin's little body with Your healing grace."

Early the next morning, the phone rang. The caller ID revealed it was the hospital. Was Austin okay? Had there been a problem in the night? Had he stopped breathing again? *Dear God . . . please.*

It was the nurse from the NICU. *"Mr. Howell?"* she asked. *"Can you and Tammye come to the hospital?"*

"Absolutely. We'll be there as fast as possible" I exclaimed. *"Is everything all right? Is Austin okay?"*

"Well . . . yes," she said. *"Everything is fine. Austin's doing great. I'm not sure what happened, but something changed last night. You need to come and get your baby. He's ready to go home with you."*

There is no question in our minds, God visited that little glass box and breathed life and health into our tiny little dreamer.

When we arrived, the nurses cautioned us that Austin wasn't *"out of the woods"* just yet. He would need to come back for breathing treatments and a long list of medications. We were told it would probably be several times a week for now, and then at regular intervals for many years. *"Go home today and enjoy this miracle,"* the nurse said.

Once home, Austin began to improve rapidly—much faster than the doctors could understand. After only one visit for *"breathing treatments and medications,"* he was released.

I'm often reminded of the words of Jesus, *"All things are possible, if you can believe."*5

> *There is no question in our minds, God visited that little glass box and breathed life and health into our tiny little dreamer.*

A storm designed by the enemy to cause destruction and defeat had lost its strength. The long night on a darkened, hopeless sea was giving way to a glimpse of *the other side.*

Austin would grow up strong and healthy, full of life and energy. A man's man. A covering to his family. A light to many. A leader of leaders.

And that *"runt"* the doctors spoke of can break a rock with a wooden spoon and no intention. Weak has never since been mentioned in the same breath with his name.

Today, Austin and I walk side by side in business, life, music, ministry and family. Many say we are identical. I've often heard people say how he wants to be like me. As much as I'd like to think that, I'd have to say it's the other way around. You see, I dream of being like him.

He's a source of great inspiration to many. A challenge to understand at times; but then again, dreamers are designed in a special way. Now, he's raising his own "little dreamers."

From time to time, I remind him of his story. How adversity attacked him from the moment he was born. I remind him, *"The enemy couldn't stop you then, and he can't stop you now. Never give up. Never stop believing. Never stop dreaming. Regardless of the storm, reach for the other side."*

Chapter 6

The Auburn Princess

It was December of 1992. We were preparing for Austin's second Christmas. The year had been a special year. The church was growing larger still. We had just purchased property and were preparing to expand the ministry. Once again, it seemed like everything was perfect.

Sadly, it wasn't.

Tammye's mother had not been feeling well. We didn't know why, but the doctors would soon tell us.

She had been diagnosed with a very aggressive ovarian cancer.

How could this be? She was too young to be sick. Barely fifty years old and otherwise in good health. Could they treat it? Could they operate? What should we do?

The questions of uncertainty began to flood in with the power of a hurricane. The news was overwhelming.

First and foremost, we needed to pray. As people of faith, we believed in healing. We've seen many people healed of various diseases and afflictions and we've witnessed numerous miracles. *"She will be healed!"* we declared.

Tammye had a unique relationship with her mother. Much like many mother-daughter relationships, they had both good times and bad. Regrettably, the dismal days had numbered far too many. Whatever challenges they may have faced before would need to be put behind them now.

Tammye was the only child of her mom's second marriage. Joining two older siblings, a brother and sister, the family blended together to become one. Surviving on meager means, life was somewhat simple even for rural Oklahoma. The routine consisted of nine to five's at the factory, church on Sunday, homegrown vegetables from the family garden and chores unending.

Garnering signature locks of auburn, Tammye not only adorned the same beautiful hair as her mother, but they also shared a vibrancy of life that seemed to captivate any room. When they laughed, strangers joined in. When they danced, the world spun beneath them. When they shopped—well, let's just say they liked to shop.

To look at one instantly gave a picture of the other. Beautiful, both inside and out. So many similarities. So many things in common.

Unfortunately, they also had a few scars. Deep wounds that opened uninvited, like glacial chasms piercing far beneath the surface of majestic beauty. Tracing behind the closed doors of family dynamics, some things were better left unspoken.

Not so different from other families, there were delicate areas they preferred not to address at Sunday dinner. In the same regard, they had spent an equal portion of their lives struggling to find resolve.

How is it that two people can love each other so much, yet falter at a whim to find peace and harmony?

Was it jealousy? Bitterness? Unforgiveness? Whatever "*it*" was, it would no longer be given the power to hold them prisoner. There was a new battle to fight, and this one mattered.

It's important to note we are not perfect people. We all have inherent design flaws. Some more obvious than others, but we all have them. I've often said, "There's only been one perfect Person, and we nailed Him to a cross."

You may be facing difficult dynamics with a family member or close friend. Of course, you love each other deeply. You just can't seem to get past a problem in your relationship. You may have tried time and again to resolve the conflict; yet, for various reasons it just won't go away.

At some point, you have to make a conscious decision to let it go. To put it in its place—in God's hands. Let Him bring healing, forgiveness and peace.

Over the years, I've witnessed a long list of people carrying life's luggage with problems that should've been dealt with in another lifetime. It's sad how many struggle through life, laden with cares they need not shoulder.

I can assure you with absolute certainty, the time will come when you will wish you had abandoned that vile of venom. Holding on to it yields nothing good. It's like being in a prison where you hold the keys. You can leave anytime, but for unfounded reasons, you elect to stay another night.

I admire those who find the courage to face their dilemmas and take ownership of any part they may have in contributing to the evil root. Life is far too fragile to harbor anything poisonous in the depths of our soul.

Jesus looked at His crucifiers and prayed, *"Father, forgive them."*[6] Upon His resurrection from the grave, He located Peter, reaffirming the love and respect they shared for each other. Peter had failed miserably, denying that he even knew his best friend, Jesus. In a moment of weakness, he did the unthinkable. Yet, Jesus refused to let Peter live with the regret of this decision.

This type of forgiveness is life-giving. It's incomparable to any force we know. Its intrinsic value releases freedom unparalleled. It would serve us well to embrace it on a larger scale.

Tammye and her mother needed to put behind them anything that may have been in question to that point as her mother stepped into the fight for her life. Tammye's mother not only wanted, she needed her baby girl by her side.

The following months consisted of a radical surgery and painful treatments. The once vibrant locks of auburn had now vanished. The once enthusiastic, glistening beauty of life now sheltered in a cape of weakness.

Each new day was more important than the last. Grace was now more than a short prayer before the family meal. Family gatherings, holidays and the occasional shopping trip had suddenly become priceless.

Austin was too young to fully grasp the magnitude of the moment. He only knew that his Mema Pat was sick in some way. Regardless of how much pain she may have been experiencing, she never refused a hug from any of her grandbabies. She would put on a smile and pretend that everything was just fine, even though it wasn't.

Her fight was valiant and her courage was admirable. In 1993, doctors gave her the news so many had prayed to hear, *"You are cancer free!"*

Oh, the elation. The joy. The relief. Thank You, God, for healing and peace. It was time for a celebration.

The surgeries, medications and treatments had ravaged her body. She was now a shell of the woman she once was. Not only was the cancer gone, but so were vital organs that had to be removed. Also missing was the dignity that once carried her vibrancy.

On the other hand, she was also no longer burdened with inner struggles that had secretly tormented her for a lifetime.

There is something solemn about facing a life-threatening crisis. Whether running from a storm of historic proportions or staring into the eyes of the abyss, cataclysmic events have a sobering effect.

Regretfully, it often takes a calamitous moment to inspire us to the purity of life. The soldier rescued on the battlefield. The skydiver requiring his emergency chute. The real time proving of an officer's bullet-proof vest. All share an acute awareness that life is fragile.

In an instant, everything that matters in life rises to the front of our consciousness. Words such as, *"I love you"* hold a power unmatched. *"I appreciate you"* magically brightens the darkest night. *"I forgive you"* yields an immeasurable and unparalleled freedom. The fruition of *the other side* instantaneously becomes a paradise realized.

This too was true for Tammye and her mom. At last, they were able to enjoy the treaty they had often pursued.

The elation would be short lived, however. Somewhere around the holidays of 1994, doctors revealed those painful words, "The cancer is back."

In a heartbeat, it was like all the air was sucked from the room. What now? How bad is it? We will fight it. We beat it once, and we'll beat it again. Our resolve may have been determined, but we weren't the ones with the diagnosis.

The next few months yielded many ups and downs. Tammye was adamant that nothing would deter her from helping in every way possible. It was a complex scenario, partly due to the fact that we lived two hours away and were responsible for a large ministry. Nonetheless, she pledged never to miss an opportunity to be by her mother's side.

Disease may have been ravaging a physical body, but unprecedented healing was taking place between a dying mother and her daughter. Their greatest beauty was more alive than ever before. Unequaled by any force known to exist, love had bonded them in ways beyond compare.

It was the last days of July, 1995, on the heels of Austin's fourth birthday. Family and friends gathered closer and more frequently around Patricia, anticipating the obvious.

Tammye felt it was important to stay with her mom for the entire week. So we made the necessary arrangements and drove the two hours from Oklahoma City to Muskogee.

Upon our arrival that Monday evening, Tammye's mom asked if she and I could talk, alone. To this day, I've never shared publicly the details of our conversation. Only for the purpose of helping someone else find strength and courage do I take any liberty now.

As she lay in bed, weakened and frail, she shared with me delicate moments from her life. Stories that carried years of pain, much more painful than the horrid disease she now battled. She told of mistakes that caused sorrow to those she loved the most. Grudges and grievances rooted in generational misguidance. Poisonous conversations that could never be undone.

It was unclear as to why I was chosen as the urn to carry these ashes. What was profoundly clear was the inner cleansing which took place as it washed away decades of hidden pain and undisclosed regret. It seemed as if each tear carried solace and liberty. As she prepared for her greatest journey yet, she had summoned the strength to cut away the anchor and free herself from a harbor incapable of holding her vessel any longer.

On Friday of that same week, I returned to Muskogee to pick up Tammye. Once again, a private conversation was requested for my ears only. Doctors had given up hope of any recovery. Hospice had been called. It was no longer "if," but "when."

This time, my chat with Patricia was a bit more resolute. To my amazement, there was no sorrow nor sadness in her voice. There was, however, a deep sense of tranquility. *"I'm ready"* she yielded, with a feeble breath. *"I've taken care of everything that we talked about before and I'm ready to go. I can go in peace and know that everything is okay. It's all been taken care of."*

Through the tears, we prayed and thanked God for His amazing grace that is ever present to cover and comfort us.

With heavy hearts, Tammye, Austin and I prepared to head back to Oklahoma City. The embrace between Tammye and her mom seemed to last forever. Then again, we knew eternity was waiting, closer than ever before.

When we returned to Patricia's bedside, just three days later, her breath was weak and shallow. The glistening dew was now gone from her eyes. The pinkish hue in her skin had been replaced by an ashy stain. She had made her most difficult and arduous decisions days before. Now, it was only to wait. Like a princess preparing to be swept away, she waited for the angels on whose wings she would soon fly.

On Tuesday morning, August 1, 1995, holding the hand of her baby girl, she set sail for *the other side;* at peace with God, her daughter and herself.

Rest in peace, Patricia June Girty. Your courage will never be forgotten.

A few days after her passing, Austin told us that Mema Pat came and talked to him. When we inquired as to how this could be, he explained that she came to him in a dream. He further explained that she had told him she was okay. She was no longer sick, but in heaven with Jesus. She told him she loved him very much and would see him again some day.

Until this time, he had been very troubled about her passing. After this, he was a happy little four-year-old boy again. He still missed her, but he was otherwise happy.

It is beyond me to explain or understand the dynamics of how something like this could happen, except to say that I believe it did. Children have an acute sense about them, particularly in spiritual matters. I've encountered many children who have given detailed accounts of spiritual matters that had no natural explanation.

On a brighter note, twenty-two years later, Austin's second child, Miss Hollyn June was born on August 1, 2017, the anniversary of her great-grandmother's triumphant arrival on *the other side.* It is a day that is forever shared in the legacy of our family.

Austin's son Graham was dancing and playing in the hallway of their house when he was about two and a half years old. (The same house in which Patricia lived and later passed.) It was clear that he was talking to someone; having a vivid and pleasant conversation. When asked with whom he spoke, he politely replied, *"Mema Pat."*

Some things are simply beyond our scope of understanding and are impossible to explain. Call me crazy, but I believe God allows rare and inexplicable events like this far more than we are willing to admit.

Chapter 7

Humpty Dumpty

As you can imagine, the death of Tammye's mom had a significant impact on our little family. The rise and setting of the sun seemed to carry a different glow.

Flowers in Patricia's garden now danced with a heavenly heartbeat. The hummingbirds she loved to feed seemed more abundant than ever, whisking here and there, searching for the nectar of life. The radiant canteens of juicy divine now required someone else to fill their void. It seemed that even they knew their morning dance with the auburn princess had somehow changed.

Even still, our lives would have to go on.

If Humpty Dumpty sat on that wall, why, oh why, did we have to fall?

The church seemed stronger than ever. The new facility was overflowing. Our ministry continued to expand. We were holding multiple services every weekend and participating in strategic plants of new churches. We traveled with our music; broadcast on multiple radio and TV outlets; developed new

If Humpty Dumpty sat on that wall, why, oh why, did we have to fall?

curriculum; hosted conferences; conducted crusades and humanitarian outreaches, several of which were in foreign countries, etc., etc.

Oh yes, and in the midst of all the business, our family was grieving over the loss of Tammye's mother.

Remember those "time bandits" I spoke of earlier? They were alive and well. Their teeth had sunk deep into the vein of my daily schedule. As organized as I sought to be, it was still terribly difficult to manage all the things which cried out for a piece of my life.

Though it was a torrid pace, I was young and thought, *"I can handle this."* Unfortunately, my marriage needed more attention than I was giving it.

It's foolish to think you can neglect the thing that is most important in your life and yet expect it to thrive.

As much as a delicate flower needs water to survive, so too, our relationships are reliant on the attentive care that once nurtured them to life. Families are a micro community, and they require constant attention to help ensure prolonged health and happiness.

> *It's foolish to think you can neglect the thing that is most important in your life and yet expect it to thrive.*

I understood this. I was teaching this principle on multiple fronts. If anyone should have exemplified this, it was me.

The problem often arises when we get so busy "doing" that we forget what's most important to be done. Like turning off the cell phone during dinner. Like coming home to your family and actually being engaged with them while you're there.

I watch today as families fade away to different parts of their homes, all doing something they feel is good and purposeful, yet doing none of it together. A television in every room, so everyone can watch their favorite show; yet never watching a program together. On Sunday, every family member drives alone in their own vehicle to church simply because they can't find a common time to leave together. *"I'll meet you at the restaurant. I'll see you when we get home later."*

At times, it's as if we are mere roommates or business partners in life rather than a singular member of love, joined by our hearts.

Jesus commented in Matthew 19:5-6 NLT, *"A man leaves his father and mother and is joined to his wife, and the two are united into one. Since they are no longer two but one, let no one split apart what God has joined together."*

How can we truly be "one" when we live such distinctly separate lives? Just because we are under the same roof is not indicative of unity. Both of our names on the mortgage says nothing to the bond of matrimony.

We want to take a stand about protecting our family from outsiders, yet more times than not, the greatest war is waged from within.

I'm not attacking the beauty of individuality. We each are created with a divine purpose and possess God-given talents that enhance every part of our existence. The problem arises in marriage when we seek to serve ourselves, as individuals, above the greater whole of our union.

Lucifer was a beautiful being, created with very specific gifts. Yet, he set himself to ascend above the deity that had set him in order. His demise and subsequent fall were prolific. Still today, he serves up his venom on every platter. Convincing one after another what's best for them is all that matters.

It troubles me to hear couples that have been married for many years arrive at a conclusion to divorce. What's even more troubling is the varied reasons offered up. In particular, many are convinced they need to be in a different relationship, or worse yet, all alone, sighting *"I just need to do what's best for me."* It's certainly admirable to maintain a vigilance monitoring our personal well-being. However, relationship is not about "our" needs. It's about serving the needs of the one we're in relationship with.

Granted, marriage may not be for everyone and divorce is not the eternal damnation to darkness; but to believe that your needs are what matter most is akin to pegasus flying too close to the sun.

In Greek mythology, Icarus is the son of the master craftsman Daedalus, the creator of the Labyrinth. Icarus and his father attempt to escape from Crete by means of wings that his father constructed from feathers and wax. Icarus' father warns him first of complacency and then of hubris, charging that he fly neither too low nor too high so the sea's dampness would not clog his wings nor the sun's heat melt them. However, Icarus ignored his father's instructions not to fly too close to the sun. Thus, the wax in his wings melted and he fell into the sea. *(Wikipedia.)*

We've become a society of ME. Make ME happy. What can you do for ME? What's best for ME? Look at ME. Wait, let me post that again. Look at ME. Here's a pic of ME with my hair up. Now here's a pic of ME with my hair down. Oh, and here's a pic of ME in a cap.

It sounds horrid to consider, but this is who our society has become. Individuals, to the point of losing focus of common goals and shared perspective. If our politicians ever learn how to work together in unity, we'll solve world hunger, have no taxes and the streets will be paved with gold. Yip, that would be heaven.

Unfortunately for my family, the wax on our wings was about to melt.

Turmoil and division had developed in our home, and it was seething into everything we touched. No longer were things turning to gold. It was more like rust. Confidence in our ability to lead was waning. Futility seemed to preach louder than my sermons, and the feathers had begun to fall from our wings.

Every day became a struggle. Finances began to falter. Attendance was dropping with rapid succession, week by week. Delicate questions were being asked as people probed and pointed.

> *Unfortunately for my family, the wax on our wings was about to melt.*

For the first time in our life, it seemed no one wanted to be around us. It felt like we had some highly contagious disease.

Finally, the phone stopped ringing and invitations stopped coming. Friends seemed invisible, and life was anything but good.

Our once happy, healthy family had found its way into the midst of a storm-tossed sea. *"Who is this woman I married? Who is this jerk she has for a husband? What are we doing? Should we divorce? Should we leave the church?"* These questions and thousands more swirled through our minds like tornadoes in the Oklahoma spring.

We tried to convince ourselves we had what everyone wanted, even though it was becoming quite obvious, no one wanted what we had.

In the fall of 1997, I travelled to Ukraine to help with a crusade and humanitarian outreach, knowing all the while I may not have anything to come home to. Purposefully hiding my inner fears and frustrations, I held my wings high and pretended they were as good as new. Gracefully, some very dear friends encouraged me otherwise.

I had known for months that it was time to leave Oklahoma City, but to actually put it in motion was another matter. I remembered what one of my mentors taught me years before. **"If God can speak to me about it, He can also speak to my wife."** I prayed and asked God to confirm it in Tammye, then give us the courage to find help for our failing family.

> *We tried to convince ourselves we had what everyone wanted, even though it was becoming quite obvious, no one wanted what we had.*

It was on a phone call while I was in Ukraine that I first heard her say the words, *"I think we should resign the church."* As painful as it was to hear those words, I knew it was time and so did she. We weren't helping anyone, and wherever we thought we were leading people couldn't have been in the right direction.

Somewhere deep inside, I was relieved.

It's often difficult for us to embrace change, especially when it challenges our comfort zone. There is a popular line of thought that people don't want change. Contrary to that statement, I believe they do; but only when they see the benefit and how it directly affects them in a positive way.

Consider a few things along this line:

- No one WANTS to change a flat tire at night in the rain; but it may be required if you want to get to your destination.

- No one WANTS to see a beautiful day end, but we understand that it must in order to start another beautiful day tomorrow.

- No one WANTS to go through labor and delivery, but the baby is well worth the pain.

Change typically comes down to a matter of perspective. Depending on your perspective, you may or may not want change. Likewise, you may or may not see the need for it.

This is quite often a challenge for leaders whether pastors, businessmen, coaches or bankers. Everything points in the direction that says change is needed, but we hesitate to go through the process of changing.

Entrepreneurs understand the need for change. Successful people understand the need for change. A new paradigm can be a very healthy venture, particularly if you're on the right side of the change.

Everyone is familiar with the story of Swiss watchmakers who refused to embrace new technology. Unfortunately for them, they went from owning 90 percent of the market to owning only a fraction. All because they refused to embrace change.

What is the lesson to be learned? Stop fighting change. Stop being so arrogant to think that everything will stay the same. The world is constantly changing; and if you refuse to change, you will be left behind wondering what happened.

> *One of the greatest revelations we could ever hope to acquire is to understand when a season begins and when it ends.*

Ecclesiastes says there is a season for everything. One of the greatest revelations we could ever hope to acquire is to understand when a season begins and when it ends. Once we recognize this, we should pray for courage to embrace the new season and earnestly consider the changes it brings.

Jesus taught a powerful principle regarding change when He taught about the need to put new wine in new wineskins. He revealed how putting new wine in old wineskins will not work. The old wineskin will break because it is no longer pliable. It would serve us well to remember this revelatory verity. Moving into a new season is easily likened to this parable. A changing season will also require changes in other areas of our life.

This was the case as we left Oklahoma City. Our season there had come to an end. Regardless of how much anyone wanted it to continue, it was over. We knew it. The church knew it, and we just needed to embrace it.

We were falling apart like Humpty Dumpty. We desperately needed a change. We not only needed new wine, we also needed a new wineskin. As the expression goes, *"Change nothing and nothing changes."*

Prayerfully, a new season and strategic changes would bring a fresh start and a new sense of purpose. It wasn't the end of our destiny, just the end of a season.

Chapter 8

Trailer Trash

As fast as our rise to prominence, so too was our fall. Tempers flared, incendiary comments hurled like fireballs over the bough of our vessel. *"You're not welcome here any longer. You need to leave!"*

How could it have come to this point? Not only was this intrusive and abrasive mind-set wreathing with disdain throughout our congregation, it had also invaded our home.

We had never been in a place like this before. We were definitely in uncharted waters.

We prepared, as best we could, to depart Oklahoma City in peace, hoping for the opportunity to retain at least some sense of dignity. We met with our board of directors, addressed the congregation and prepared to transition out.

Wading through a short list of open invitations, I decided it would be best to return to my hometown of Muskogee, Oklahoma, and take an associate roll with the church I had grown

> *We had never been in a place like this before. We were definitely in uncharted waters.*

up in. The pastor was a dear friend who had also travelled on the recent trip to Ukraine. He, as much as anyone, knew the fragile thread that was holding us together.

Expecting Tammye to join me in this new role, I was not prepared for her next comments. *"I don't want to go back to Muskogee with you. In fact, I'm not sure I even want to be married to you anymore."*

If it wasn't bad before, it certainly was now. I'm not sure what I was even thinking at that moment. I only remember crying—a lot.

I had given every breath since I was just a little boy to try and help others find a better way of life, and my reward seemed to be a failing marriage. If this was the reward for ministry, then I didn't want anything to do with it.

> ❧
>
> **If this was the reward for ministry, then I didn't want anything to do with it.**

Perhaps it wasn't fair to blame the church or ministry, but I felt I needed to blame someone, and they were the easy target.

It's important to note, ministry is hard just as many other forms of business. I remember my first day of Bible college. They taught us how to spell ministry.

W-O-R-K.

Sadly, I have witnessed many who have left the ministry, never to return. Their life shattered. Their dreams abandoned and their families in ruin.

Even more disheartening, their children often refuse to have any significant interaction with ministry or the church. Some even go as far as to claim they no longer believe in God.

Though often painful and frustrating, ministry is not the culprit of this disdain. More importantly, neither is God.

Reluctantly, we packed the truck and headed east with our tail tucked between our legs. Sadness, fatigue, frustration, anger, bitterness, hopelessness, despair . . . they all seemed to pack up and climb in the truck with us. Thankfully, Tammye found the courage to trudge along as well. She was a reluctant passenger, but she was there.

> ❧
> *Though often painful and frustrating, ministry is not the culprit. More importantly, neither is God.*

We had no place to live and no money left to buy or rent a home. We were several hundred thousand dollars in debt and couldn't even buy gas for the truck to leave town.

The church we were going to owned a small trailer house (very small). Today, most of my hotel rooms are larger than that trailer. The fact that it was located on the church property was both convenient and irritating. We were allowed to live there for free until we were financially able to do something different. That was December of 1997, and it did not look to be a Christmas we wanted to remember.

I am so grateful for the true friends that stood by us in that dark place. Those who did, certainly had a divine purpose and an eternal connection to our destiny.

There was one little lady in particular. She wasn't very tall and not very loud, but she knew how to pray. Many times, day and night, we would hear her outside of our little trailer. She would be walking around it and praying over us. She would stand against every demonic agenda that had raised its ugly head toward us. She prayed for our health, for peace in our marriage and for God's will to be done in our lives. To this day, nearly twenty years later, she is still praying over us. Today, she leads the prayer ministry in our church.

Never underestimate the power of prayer!

I was directing the worship ministry at the church; thus I had some obligations to attend to. With that in mind, the pastor was beyond gracious to afford us the freedom to strategically avoid some of the ongoings in the congregation.

> *Never underestimate the power of prayer!*

Our adjustment the first few months was painfully challenging. On many occasions Tammye and Austin never attended the services. Austin could typically be found hiding out in my office. While he didn't know all the details, he was smart enough to know things weren't good in our home. In his mind, the church was the greatest blame for his pain and he wanted nothing to do with those new people.

As much as we hated that little trailer, it really wasn't all that bad. It forced us to look in the mirror. It forced us to address our issues and face our problems. We couldn't run and hide in the back of the house, primarily because there was no back of the house.

It allowed us to gather our finances and make plans to get back on our feet. Little by little, slowly and deliberately we were gaining our strength back.

Tammye found a house she thought we should buy. When she first told me about it, I laughed. How could we buy a house? We had no money for a down payment. We were up to our eyeballs in debt, and let's not forget, we weren't sure we were going to stay together.

Ordinarily, I would advise against such a significant decision when a marriage is in such turmoil. Somewhere deep inside, however, it seemed that God was working a new miracle.

We agreed to put a contract on the house. When it was accepted, I remember still thinking, *"Where are we going to get the money for closing?"* As the closing date drew near, crazy things began to happen. For no apparent reason, people began giving us money. People we didn't know sent checks in the mail. They said they had no apparent reason for doing it, but felt like they were supposed to give.

Sure enough, we ended up with just enough money to close on our new house. Strangely, it was right around the corner from our first apartment. Stranger still, the entire eight years we spent in Oklahoma City, we never bought a house. Every time we tried, either the deal would mysteriously fall through or the Holy Spirit would move us in a different direction. In hindsight, had we owned a home in Oklahoma City, we may have never moved back to Muskogee.

I never believed I would say this, but I'm glad we moved back.

It may have been *the other side* of the world from where we wanted to be; but nonetheless, it was *the other side* and that's a good place to be.

Chapter 9

Last Call

When we left Oklahoma City, we felt like God was leading us to take two years and dedicate that time to our family. There was something very specific about that time frame. It seemed to resonate loudly in our spirit.

Two years! Two years!! Two years!!!

Okay, I get it. Two years.

That may not sound like a hard thing for some, but for us it was. We had been extremely busy for the past ten years. To simply stop doing all that we were doing for two years would be difficult at best. I don't mean to sound like we weren't going anywhere or doing anything, but in obedience to that word, we would be engaged in nothing significant. No revivals, no crusades, no mission trips, no traveling. Instead we would keep to a very limited schedule.

The reason seemed rather obvious; to spend time with our family. We understood it was important to rebuild our relationship and that would only happen if we stayed focused. We can't give our attention to all the other areas and still expect to have success at home. After all, we learned our lesson in Oklahoma City—hopefully.

Honestly, taking a little time off was a good thing. We were able to spend quality time together as a family. As a bonus, we were able to enjoy the company of our extended family—which we enjoyed. (Sadly, this is not true for every family.)

Generally speaking, our family is very close. During this season we spent time in activities such as fishing with my dad and brother. Special lunches with Mom and dinner with Tammye's dad. Austin played sports with two of his cousins who were more like brothers than cousins. Not to mention, Austin was able to spend a lot of time with my parents and Tammye's dad. He had never been able to do this while we lived in Oklahoma City.

Having lost her mother only two years earlier, this season also gave Tammye the opportunity to spend more time with her father, Tom, or Papa Tom as Austin called him. They had always been very close, but this gave them the chance to grow even closer. We had been in Oklahoma City for nearly eight years during which visits were short and rare.

I had always carried a tremendous admiration for Tom. From the very first time we met, I fell in love with him. Not just because I wanted to marry his daughter. He is quite simply one of the finest human beings I've ever had the privilege of knowing.

When he and Pat were first married, he not only received her as his wife, but also her two children from a previous marriage. He accepted responsibilities that were not his. He raised both children as if they were his own with the same care, provisions and love. This was an admirable trait.

When Tammye came along, he continued to provide the same care and provision to the entire family—although it is quite possible that she was the apple of his eye.

They were inseparable. Always together working, playing, laughing. Anything that Tom was doing, Tammye wanted to be right in the middle of it. Even when they would haul hay and do chores in the summer, Tammye worked right alongside her daddy.

She even learned to drive in the hay field (which might explain a few things). When she was still a very small child, Tom would take her to haul hay. It was just the two of them out in the field. He often would put the truck in granny gear, put little Tammye behind the steering wheel and let her go. Then he would jump out of the truck as it was moving very slowly, and then walk beside the truck as he threw the hay bales on the back. Legend says "hay" wasn't the only thing he threw. He may have hurled a few misappropriate words towards the driver every now and then when she didn't follow directions. But what do you expect? She couldn't even reach the pedals!

Regardless, they were together. Few things made him as proud as being with his baby girl whether they were out in the barn, milking the cows or going to get an Icee — they were together. Father and daughter, inseparable.

After moving back to Muskogee, Tammye drew even closer to Tom as did Austin. Every day they talked on the phone, sharing life with all its twists and turns. On Friday nights, you could always find Tammye and her dad together at dinner. On Saturdays, he and Austin would go off to the farm for another life lesson learned. Sunday meant Tammye and her dad got to worship and pray together as church was a high priority.

In November of '99, we convinced Tom to go with us to Oklahoma City for Thanksgiving dinner with some very dear friends. We had such a great time that Thanksgiving. I will forever be glad we made that trip. Little did we know the series of events right around the corner.

Before we could hang lights on the Christmas tree, Tammye's whole world would be shattered.

As good as things were going at home, we still had a few dilemmas to deal with. From time to time, tempers would flare and things would get a bit heated. We were definitely doing better, but still had work to do.

Just a couple weeks beyond that great family trip for Thanksgiving, things hit a snag at home. Tammye and I got into a terrible argument. Honestly, I don't remember the details of why we were fighting. I do remember being frustrated and thinking, *"Can we please just figure out how to get along without fussing and fighting all the time?"*

It was Saturday night in early December. Tammye and I were so wound up from arguing, we decided to sleep in separate bedrooms that night.

Somewhere around midnight or so, the phone rang. Neither of us wanted to get out of bed and go answer the phone. So we let it ring. Truthfully, we were just being stubborn. Childish is probably a better word, even though I can think of at least a thousand ugly words that describe how we were acting that night. Pitiful may say it best.

In those days, we had an answering machine. The kind that would answer the phone after a few rings, then record a message onto a small tape. In many ways, this was the first round of caller ID's. When the caller would leave a message, you could hear it over a little speaker, thus you might know who was calling and either pick up the phone or just let it go.

I could hear from the bedroom, it sounded like Tom. I immediately got out of bed to go to the phone; but by the time I got there, he had already hung up. I went to wake up Tammye and tell her he had called. For him to be calling this late seemed very strange indeed.

Tom had left a message letting us know that he wasn't feeling well.

We immediately tried calling him back, but there was no answer. Concerned, we decided it would be best to go to his house and check on him.

My brother lived in the same neighborhood as we did, so we dropped Austin off with him and made our way to Tom's house. He lived outside of the city, so it was normally about a fifteen to twenty minute drive. I drove as fast as I possibly could. Though we arrived in only a few minutes, it seemed like hours.

When we got to his house, the gate was locked. Tom's truck was in the driveway, so it appeared he was still there. We climbed over the fence and ran to the house, frantically knocking on the doors and calling his name. There was no answer and no sign that anyone was home.

We scoured the property. In a panic, we shouted his name, searching everywhere we could think to look. EMT's had also arrived. (We had called them from our cell phone while on our way.) They also were searching desperately for any sign of Tom.

After what seemed like an eternity, we received a phone call from the neighbor. Apparently, Tom had locked up his house, checked on his animals, locked the gate, then walked a quarter mile to his neighbor's house to ask them to drive him to the hospital, because he wasn't feeling well.

We immediately drove to the local hospital to find him in the ER. Much to our disappointment, we were informed that he was having a heart attack. There was a frenzy of effort around him. To the untrained eye, it seemed like organized chaos. Valiantly, the medical team was making every effort possible to save him.

Finally, the doctors allowed us to see him. Tammye immediately went to his side. Taking his calloused hand in hers, she gently leaned over the bedside, strategically placing a daughter's kiss on his cheek. *"I love you, Daddy,"* she whispered softly in his ear.

At this point, tears were flowing uncontrollably. Tom was unresponsive and lay motionless. He was alive, barely; and struggling.

After an hour or so in the ER, the doctors informed us they needed to transport him to Tulsa where he would be able to receive more intensive care.

There was a problem, however. Due to weather issues and thick fog, they could not fly the Life-Flight helicopter. He would have to make the trip by ambulance. The helicopter could fly there in minutes. The ambulance would take an hour at best. Time was not on his side.

One more time, Daddy's little girl clutched his hand and told him how much she loved him. With a kiss and a prayer, he was in the ambulance and on his way.

Through the dense fog, the siren and lights seemed to radiate into a void of helplessness. *"Faster, drive faster!"* we cried as we followed close behind.

Upon arriving at the hospital in Tulsa, we could see a flurry of activity in the back of the ambulance. Tom had gone into full cardiac arrest. They were using every method available to save him.

We were ushered into a small family room as they moved him from the ambulance to the ER. Minutes passed in what seemed like an eternity.

When we arrived at the hospital, some very dear friends from Oklahoma City were waiting on us. Their embrace was priceless. Their friendship unparalleled. This was the same family that first welcomed us to Oklahoma City. Over the years, they became more than friends. They were family.

The night was fading into the morning. It had been an unforgettable night of gut-wrenching pain. Though most of the sting was emotional, it seemed to writhe deep into our soul. Why didn't we answer the phone when Tom called? What if we could've gotten to him sooner? If only we could've talked to him, even if just for a moment. Was there something else he wanted to tell Tammye? The barrage of questions and emotional attacks seemed unending. Still, the most important question on our minds was whether or not Tom would survive this horrid assault.

Ten years before, Tom underwent quadruple bypass heart surgery. At that time, the doctors expressed that he may need additional procedures after about ten years. After that surgery and recovery, Tom often expressed that he only had ten years left to live. Though this was not at all what the doctors had said, it was certainly what he believed. The closer he got to that ten-year anniversary, the more intentional he became about certain matters.

With determined resolution, he made sure all his legal paperwork was in place and up to date. He routinely visited family and friends, never leaving without first telling them how much he loved and appreciated them. It seemed as if he knew his appointment with eternity was close at hand.

Only a few weeks before this attack, Tom picked up Austin and took him to the 'old home place' as Tom called it. It was the land his family received in the Native American allotment from the government. The land Tom grew up on learning to hunt, fish and farm. He had suddenly decided he needed to rebuild Austin's small fort. The same fort we had built and then transported from Oklahoma City. It was a special day between Tom and his one and only grandson. Only God could truly know the importance of that day.

As we sat in the tiny little room at the hospital, we did the only thing we knew to do, pray. The air was thick with an uneasiness that presented itself on every tick of the clock. Tick, tick, tick. The small clock hanging on the wall seemed to scream louder and louder with every beat. Seconds turned to minutes and minutes turned to an eternity of frantically waiting.

Though it seemed like forever, after only a short time, there was a knock at the door of our little room. It was the doctor. The look on his face immediately revealed the pain of his coming words.

"I'm saddened to tell you, Tom didn't make it."

His words fell like bricks on the glass pallet of our heart. All hope was immediately shattered. Eternity had come calling again. In a matter of only four and a half short years, heaven had received both of Tammye's parents. Tears flowed freely as we called on God to somehow help us through this agony.

Strangely, it was in this moment of grief that I was reminded of something most unique. That day marked two years exactly to the day since we left the church in Oklahoma City.

Now, more than ever, I was thankful we had gone back to Muskogee. Thankful for Friday night dinners with Tom and family lunches after church on Sunday. We were especially thankful for that timely trip to Oklahoma City for Thanksgiving dinner, as it was our last holiday with Tom.

Those two years suddenly became more valuable than anything we could've imagined. The time Tammye and Austin were able to spend with Tom would be treasured throughout eternity.

God had supernaturally directed our steps back to our home, partly for this time. Who, but God, could've known how things would turn out? Perhaps those two years had been a special gift of His grace.

It was unimaginable that our **last call** from Tom would have occurred in such a way. The last words Tammye heard from her father were on the answering machine, *"Tammye, this is your dad. I'm not feeling well. I need to talk to you."*

These words have painfully echoed through our broken hearts ever since that dreadful night. Equally painful was the frustration of knowing that we didn't answer the phone, because we were fighting.

It's impossible for us to know when heaven will call someone's name. Thus, it is imperative to always consider the possibility that a conversation or holiday dinner with the family may hold more significance than we realize.

I've often encountered families who chose not to share their holidays together. Families who refused to gather on a routine basis for lunch or maybe just to have ice cream and visit. It is heartbreaking to witness, regardless of the many reasons why families choose this path.

> *"Take time to be with your family."*

If you get nothing else from these pages, hear me when I say, "Take time to be with your family."

After a loved one is gone, you will always remember the last conversation you had with them. The last meal. The last trip. The last embrace. I can promise you with great assurance, we have never forgotten *the last call* we received from Tom.

Currently, Austin is raising his family in the house Tom built many years ago. Sadly, Austin's children will only know Papa Tom through pictures and stories. I'm sure he would be pleased to know that they are being raised with a great appreciation for the Cherokee culture he held so dear to his heart.

One day, we will surely meet again on *the other side*.

Godspeed, Thomas Martin Girty.

In the words of his native Cherokee tongue . . .

Donvdagohvi. (Until we meet again.)

Chapter 10

A New Season

Our world was obviously shaken with Tom's passing. Suddenly, our petty little arguments no longer held the same importance. Life would never be the same again. Hopefully we had learned an unforgettable lesson about letting our anger and our emotions rule (or ruin) our lives.

We determined it was time to get closure and find a way to rebuild our family.

It was time to fully realize our potential and allow God to use us in the way He wanted.

It was the fall of 2000. Upon returning from a meeting in Ohio, I was scheduled to attend a meeting with the board of directors at the church where we were currently serving. I remember praying with Tammye that evening before leaving the house. There was already a great deal of transition happening in the church. We were prayerfully considering whether or not we needed to be the next to transition out.

It was time to fully realize our potential and allow God to use us in the way He wanted.

As I left the house, I remember telling Tammye, *"I'm really not sure what we need to do nor where we need to go. I feel like I will have the answer this evening."*

The men who served on the church board were good men and were attempting to fulfill their responsibilities to the church. I had known most all of them for many years. In fact, I remember when most of them were saved, and at one time or another I had taught Bible classes they attended.

The lead pastor had given notice that he was leaving to be a missionary. This left an opening in the pastorate. I wasn't sure I was the one to lead the church, nor was I sure they wanted me to. I was confident that God would take care of us, and I was willing to serve in whatever capacity He directed.

As I walked into the board room, I remember feeling an incredible peace come over me. It was as if God had wrapped His arms around me and said, *"Tonight is the last time you will meet with these men in regards to serving this church. It's time for you to leave. Let them do whatever they feel is best for this church. You need to make other plans with your family."*

> *It's time for you to leave. Let them do whatever they feel is best for this church.*

I greeted the men. We had a brief visit about the business of the church, then I offered my resignation. I shared that it had been a great privilege to serve my home church. I greatly appreciated their hospitality, particularly as they had allowed my family a place to heal. I prayed there were no hard feelings about my departure. We'd been friends for many years, and I wanted it to remain that way.

I was asked if I had plans of starting another church in town to which I answered honestly, *"At this time, I really don't know what I'm going to do."* This was completely the truth. I had no idea where I was going nor how I would even be able to feed my family and pay my bills.

I further responded that I have been in the ministry for many years, and it is the profession I have been called to. Regardless of what I decided to do or where I chose to go, I promised that I would never knowingly do anything to harm this church, or any other for that matter. After all, this was my home church. It was where I grew up. My family had served in this church for nearly fifty years.

Truthfully, I was a bit disappointed that I would no longer be serving my home church in any official capacity. For whatever reason, I knew God had released me. Beyond that, they weren't begging me to stay.

During the two years that I had most recently served here, I followed God's will, submitted to the lead pastor and served the congregation as best I could. Upon leaving Oklahoma City and coming back to Muskogee, there were several things in particular God had spoken to me. I had given great attention to each area, regardless of how difficult it may have been. At times, it was incredibly difficult, but I followed His directions.

It was what happened after the meeting that really had an impact on the future of our family. When I arrived home, Tammye wanted to know how the meeting went. I told her the basics, then I told her I had resigned my position with the church. I also informed her that I didn't know where our next paycheck would come from other than from God. He would most definitely have to supply it for us.

Feeling drained from the long day and intense emotional roller-coaster ride, I decided to spend some time in prayer. As I was praying,

I heard the voice of the Holy Spirit say something very powerful to me. Something very distinct.

"Because you have been faithful to the things that I asked of you, I am going to bless you in this next season. **Wherever you want to go . . .** *I'll bless you."*

I had never heard anything like this before. On one hand it was very comforting. On the other, it was a bit unsettling. I didn't know where I wanted to go. I wasn't sure of the best move for our family.

> ❧
>
> *"Because you have been faithful to the things that I asked of you, I am going to bless you in this next season. Wherever you want to go . . . I'll bless you."*

I decided to ask Tammye and Austin. We would make the decision together. I thought surely they would say Dallas or Nashville, or any place on Mars; just not this place.

When I asked Austin, he said he wanted to stay in Muskogee so he could be close to his cousins and my parents. Hmmm . . . well, okay. I guess I can understand that.

What about Tammye? I knew for a fact she hated this town as much as I did. We often referred to it as Nineveh.

There was one particular time shortly after we arrived back in Muskogee, we were sitting in our vehicle downtown. We were so miserable. We absolutely despised this horrid town. We actually rolled down the windows, stuck our heads out, looked up to the sky and screamed at God, *"WHY DID YOU BRING US HERE?"*

Interestingly, He responded with His ever so gentle embrace, *"Until you accept where I've brought you, I can't take you anywhere else. This is your home for now. Once you accept this place, then I can bless you."* After that day, we began to say (by faith, many times), *"Thank You, God, for bringing us here. This is a great place to live. We love it here."*

Well, we didn't completely agree with what we were saying, but we were speaking it out by faith. Surely, now that we had a chance to leave, we would do exactly that. That seemed like an easy decision.

I could understand Austin's response to stay close to family. After all, he was born in Oklahoma City and had only lived in Muskogee for a couple years. He really liked being able to play sports and spend time with his cousins. It was Tammye's response that really set me back.

"What did you say? I don't think I heard you correctly," I said stunned by her response to the question.

> *Until you accept where I've brought you, I can't take you anywhere else.*

When I asked her where she wanted to go, she also replied, *"I want to stay in Muskogee."*

Well, that was totally unexpected. I never thought she'd say that.

We decided to pray about it that night and over the next few days. Remembering and embracing what the Holy Spirit had said to me in prayer, we made the choice to stay in Muskogee.

This was a critical factor in the next chapter of our lives, as a new season was upon us. Many times over the coming years we reminded ourselves, and God, about His promise to bless us *"wherever we chose to go."* Our new season was not always easy, but I can say it was blessed.

I believe this was a crucial point in our family legacy. It meant that we would have to make a commitment to stay here longer than we had initially planned. Thankfully, we had a unique promise that we would hold on to. God had promised to bless us wherever we chose to go. Like always, He did just what He said He would do.

It's important for families to make key decisions together. It's neither fair nor wise for one person to make all the important decisions alone. Many decisions have a profound impact on the entire family. Pray about it together. Discuss it together. Even let the children offer their input. After all, it's their life too.

> *It's important for families to make key decisions together. It's neither fair nor wise for one person to make all the important decisions alone.*

I've seen too many families get into trouble when one person tried to make every decision, then force everyone else to agree with it, even when they're totally against it. This is most definitely a recipe for disaster.

When you make the decision together, then everyone has skin in the game. If things don't go as planned, everyone shares responsibility. There are no scapegoats. One person can't be blamed for forcing everyone else to go along.

Besides, forcing other people to do what you want them to do, without their agreement to do so, is called manipulation. It is also known as witchcraft.

You will never reach *the other side* if your plan to get there is through manipulation. There is no joy in manipulating other people. There is no peace in forcing others to do what you want, just so you can have your way. There is no sense of accomplishment in using unhealthy or ungodly methods to reach your goals.

Sadly, many leaders, including leaders in the church, attempt to achieve their objectives through various forms of manipulation.

I'm not only speaking of the Kool-aid drinking tragedies, where masses of people were manipulated to a point of death. I'm also addressing the subtle, innuendo, pressure-point comments often used in everyday conversations.

It's worth noting, it typically isn't one big blow that breaks a rock. It's quite often the repetitive small blows that ultimately cause it to crack. This truth is worth remembering, regardless of the venue.

A good friend once used a specific term when speaking about manipulation in the church. He called it *"white witchcraft."* He described it this way: *"Well intentioned people, manipulating others to achieve what would appear as a successful outcome."* Until that time, I had never heard this terminology.

I think it's important to define *"a successful outcome."* If your goal is to simply achieve a particular outcome, at any expense, then you may find your version of success. If your goal is to find a healthy process whereby a common goal is achieved, then you may need to look at methods that do not include manipulation.

> ✺
>
> *It's worth noting, it typically isn't one big blow that breaks a rock. It's quite often the repetitive small blows that ultimately cause it to crack.*

Manipulation is not a godly form of leadership. It is a weak display of character and identifies a person's inability to be an effective leader. Leaders who manipulate others are typically insecure. Courageous and inspiring leaders understand the importance of a unified effort in search of a common goal.

Henry Ford said it this way. *"Coming together is a beginning. Keeping together is progress. Working together is success."*

Whether in the home, the church or business, we should never coerce, pressure or attempt to manipulate people to act or react in a particular way simply because we think we know what's best. Unfortu nately, many people in positions of authority think this is the only way to lead. It is not. We should explore alternative methods of leadership and utilize the method that invokes unity and harmony. It may take more time and work to achieve the intended goal, but will generally be worth the effort in the end.

> *Courageous and inspiring leaders understand the importance of a unified effort in search of a common goal.*

I have found that casting vision is one of the most effective methods of leadership. If you can portray a clear picture of the goal and how to get there, others will inevitably embrace it and some will even go with you.

It is important to remember that people are not our property. They are not our personal soldier nor pawn in the game of life. They have choices, too. They have desires and goals. When we find people who are likeminded, share a common goal and agree on a process; we can do anything. This is true regardless of the forum: family, business, church, sports, etc.

A verse in the Bible describes it this way, *"Without vision, people perish."* (See Proverbs 29:18.) I like to say, *"Because of vision, people prosper."*

If we ever hope to reach *the other side*, we must have a clear vision of being there. If we anticipate others going with us, it will be imperative to share the vision with them so they too can move with a greater understanding and purpose.

If we are attempting to move our family in a particular direction, we need to share the vision with them of where we want to go and why. You will be surprised and possibly amazed at the success you have in doing so.

On several occasions, we have found this expressly true in rebuilding our family. Until we found agreement in a clear and concise vision of where we wanted to go, we constantly struggled to go anywhere productive. The path may have still been difficult, but at least we were in agreement, and the journey is always better this way.

Amos 3:3 says, *"Can two people walk together without agreeing on the direction?"*

A new season for us would be defined by a clear and common purpose. We were ready to embrace *a new season*.

The vision was clear and we were ready. Time would now record our steps and monitor our progress. At least we had several years of experience to draw on. To that end, we had ample experience in what *not* to do. At last our prayers had changed. We were no longer praying, "Lord, where are we going?" We finally knew the "where." If only we knew the "how."

Chapter 11

Creative Ideas

It was October of 2000 when we decided to launch a new church. Planting a new church is extremely difficult, even more so when your hometown is the potential target. This is rarely a good idea in the world of church planting.

We had spent a great deal of time in prayer about it and even though we lacked many of the usual components necessary, we felt it was the right time to move forward. We had no money to launch a church. We had no people to support the launch. We had no building, no chairs and no equipment. What we did have was a desire in our heart to do something of significance for God, and with that came vision and a promise.

We were certainly considering whether or not our hometown would be the best place to do this. We also had invitations and job offers from a handful of different places across the country. Maybe a change of scenery would be helpful for our family. Maybe a new group of friends would prove beneficial. This was definitely something that required a great deal of prayer. The one thing we were sure of was the promise we had received in prayer. *"Wherever you go, I will bless you."*

Our new season would be a challenge, yet it would also prove refreshing.

On our first Sunday, I preached the one message that you should NEVER preach on the first day of a new church launch. Sure, I spoke of vision and the kind of church we hoped to build. Then I spoke the words that I have never heard shared on the first day of a new church. *"Unless God has called you to be here with us, you can't stay. You need to go back to wherever you came from."*

> ❧
> *Our new season would be a challenge, yet it would also prove refreshing.*

There was a decent group of people for this first service; about fifty or so. They had come from all around the area. People that were familiar with our ministry, friends and even a couple of new folks that we didn't know.

We were determined to not build this church out of other churches in town, especially my home church. We felt it was important to tell people they couldn't stay unless they felt certain that God was calling them to be there, or if they had no church affiliation.

We were so emphatic of this. For the first five years of the new church, we only ran two ads in the newspaper. We had no signage directing people to the church. No radio ads. No television ads. Nothing except word of mouth and prayer.

I had prayed that God would give us *"unconventional strategies"* to reach people with the Gospel. We weren't interested in pulling unhappy people from other churches. We weren't interested in drawing the church-hopping crowd. We weren't interested in destroying other churches, just so we could build ours. We were looking for new converts or people who weren't going to church. We were looking for those who were broken and bruised. We wanted to offer hope and healing to hurting people. We had witnessed the restorative power of God in our personal lives, and we desired to share that same grace with others.

We boldly declared that God would give us facilities in which to worship. We declared that He would provide equipment and supplies for the ministry. We declared that He would supply the financial needs of both the church and our family. Most importantly, we declared that He would draw people in to the congregation. People who needed help. People who needed restoration, health and peace. People just like us. It was in this time that God gave us one of the most unique strategies I've ever been a part of.

Did you say race car?

Within a few months of starting the new church, I heard something radical and eccentric deep down in my spirit. In prayer, I felt God was directing me to sell my ATV and buy a race car. Yep, that's what I said, a race car. The kind that races on dirt.

So, that's exactly what I did. I bought an old race car (piece of junk might more adequately describe it). To me, it was more than pig iron and plastic. It was a pulpit to share the good news of Jesus.

> *Did you say race car?*

As you can probably imagine, this decision was not popular with everyone. My mother was the first to offer her disapproval. Other churches made rude and unprofessional comments about our new plan. Then, of course, there were several families attending our church who didn't see the merit in this seemingly ridiculous venture. Some even decided to leave the church because of this idea. We just blessed them to go and continued on the path we felt God had given us.

This was a significant moment in our personal lives as well as in our young church. This decision would be a defining moment for us. If it worked, we would look like innovators and creative thinkers. If it didn't, we would look like fools. I was convinced this was a God idea and I was willing to risk my life for it.

One of the first things we needed was a place to work on the car. At the time, there was a family in the church who owned a repair shop. They specialized in building off-road vehicles. They came to church sporadically, so I thought I would ask for their help. They agreed and offered to let me bring the race car to their shop. They had all the necessary tools to work on the car. It would be the perfect place.

The man who owned the shop, Bill, was very interested in this venture. He would prove to be instrumental in bringing about great success with the race car. Beyond racing, we also shared some deep conversations and built a friendship that would later prove extremely valuable.

Every week, usually on Tuesday evenings, I took the car to Bill's shop and we tried to fix, cut, weld, build, bend or invent ways to make the car work better. Each week, there would be any number of people who would casually stop by to see what was going on. Race cars are like magnets. They attract a lot of attention. In this regard, our car was no different. A lot of people were watching.

One of the best things about our Tuesday evening gathering was that most of the guys stopping by were not Christians. This may sound like a problem for some, but not for us. Those were the people we were trying to reach.

Oh, I'll agree, I didn't care for some of the language I heard or some of the off-color jokes. What I did like was that we were getting an opportunity to share Christ with people who weren't going to church anywhere. This was the first goal of ours in having a race car.

At the end of the evening, I would always offer a prayer. Suddenly, the foul language came to an abrupt end. Hats came off in reverence.

Beer cans were set aside. Heads were bowed and I began to pray. If this seems a bit out of the ordinary, you're exactly right. It was. At the same time, it proved highly effective for us.

You see, we had more in common than just an old dirty race car. We all had families who faced challenges, problems at work, marital issues, health issues, financial issues and so on. We were just men who needed help, and I was praying that God would show up and be the answer we were looking for.

Don't misunderstand me. I didn't engage in the foul language, drinking or dirty jokes. I knew I had to be different. I had to be an example, first and foremost. After all, if I acted and talked the same as people who didn't go to church and serve Christ, then what was the purpose in doing what we were doing?

A dear friend who served as our Children's Pastor had agreed to help. Pastor Randy was the crew chief, responsible for making sure the car worked. He was also responsible for keeping me safe. I was responsible for wrecking (I mean driving) the car. Hopefully together, we could share Christ along the way.

Each week when we went to the track, we would prayerfully consider where we should park in the pit area. Wherever that was, we would casually, yet intentionally, strike up a conversation with the drivers next to us. We never told anyone we were preachers. We were just a couple guys playing in the mud like everyone else.

Before the races began, as we were casually visiting with our new neighbors for the night, we would politely offer that we wanted to pray before we went out on the track. Each time, the guys would gather around and join in quietly as we prayed for safety and success.

A strange but exciting thing began to happen. These new neighbors at the track began to turn into new friends—off the track. One by one, they started showing up at church on Sunday. One by one, pledging their lives and their allegiance to Christ. It was fascinating to watch what God was doing through this unorthodox, yet creative idea. Some of these new friends have become extremely close to our family and ministry over the years.

I would be remiss if I failed to mention one family in particular. We had met a vibrant young family at the track and found ourselves parking next to each other on more than one occasion. They were always eager to pray with us and very helpful anytime we needed their assistance. He was a great racer, and we enjoyed racing (and wrecking) together for many years to come.

On one particular night, after the races, I politely posed an invitation to him, *"If you're not busy this Sunday, maybe you'd like to go to church with us."* His response was legendary.

"Hell, I go to church."

Taken back by his candor, we just laughed and left the invitation open. That Sunday morning, he and his beautiful young family found their way to our little church. Truthfully, he had been going to church most every Sunday, yet he wasn't faithfully serving God. Much like sitting in a garage can't make you a car, neither can going to church make you a Christian.

> *"Hell,*
> *I go to*
> *church."*

I am forever thankful he rededicated his heart to God that morning and has since been an integral part of the church and our family. To this day, I consider him one of my closest friends.

He not only serves as a deacon in the church, he also helps direct our humanitarian outreach, **Project Dream Seeds**. Each year thousands of school children receive assistance, food and encouragement due to his efforts.

Over the years, God caused our racing ministry to develop in ways we never could have imagined. I became known as the "Faster Pastor." No longer could we hide who we were at the track. Everyone knew us, most respected us and some even liked us. Shockingly, I somehow managed to win a few races along the way.

> *I became known as the "Faster Pastor." Everyone knew us, most respected us and some even liked us.*

Thousands came to know Christ through the efforts of CCRT (Christ Church Racing Team). Many of the track officials came to our church. My brother became the track steward and one of the most respected men in the game.

Numerous drivers and their families found a home in the congregation. I was even asked to host a local television show called "Rev'd Up with the Faster Pastor." It was solely dedicated to the local racing scene. The local newspaper once printed a full-page article about us.

An entire touring series would develop from our group. It would take us all across Oklahoma and Arkansas racing for our King. It was crazy how other tracks would call and ask if our group would come and race at their track.

We would often go, taking a whole team of children's workers complete with balloons, clowns, pictures of our cars to give away, special Bibles for racers, T-shirts, etc.

Tracks would offer us the opportunity to address the people in the grandstands and the entire group of drivers in the pits. This was truly an amazing thing.

There we were, sharing Christ with thousands of racers and fans, and it all started with one creative idea.

Our racers went on to win multiple championships and more races than we could possibly count. For many years, before I could preach on Sunday morning, we had to give a racing report from the weekend. We typically gave out a "Racer of the Week" award, honoring someone in the racing ministry for their service and achievements.

> ❧
>
> *There we were, sharing Christ with thousands of racers and fans, and it all started with one creative idea.*

At one time, our racers were involved in every type of racing imaginable; from remote control cars, go-karts, mud buggies, drag cars, ATV's and many different classes of cars on the local dirt circuit.

To this day, I have to acknowledge it was one of the most effective outreaches I have ever been a part of. It still lives on. Though not at the same level of intensity, it still continues in various places.

On most weekends, I find my way to a local racing venue to see friends, watch the next generation of champions and offer encouragement to the young men and women who grew up cheering for the Faster Pastor.

After more than forty years of music and ministry, people still ask me about racing, many times more than music or church. It truly was a creative idea that brought scores of people into the Kingdom and many of those into our local church. Some have gone on to be pastors, youth pastors, teachers, deacons and missionaries.

Regretfully, some have passed away, leaving us with fragile and delicate memories of the fun we had playing in the dirt. Many times, I have been called upon to share at memorial services for departed racers. This has been incredibly humbling, to say the least.

In the fall of 2015, we received news that one of our champions had been involved in a horrible and tragic accident. We were heartbroken to learn it was Bill, the man who had originally offered up his shop when we first began racing.

I immediately remembered a conversation he and I had. Upon returning from races in another city, he thanked me for starting that racing ministry. He continued, *"It saved my life. Without it, I would have been destined to hell."* Perspective suddenly took over the moment.

Nearly a thousand people attended his memorial service. His love for Christ most certainly spoke in his absence. Many made decisions to serve Christ because of Bill's testimony.

Recently, I was in awe when a young man who grew up in a highly successful racing family approached me with a simple request. He was not only continuing the racing legacy of his family, but was also entering into the ministry as a youth pastor. He had grown up watching me at the track and wanted to know if it was okay for him to be the new "faster pastor."

What an honor it was to hear those words of respect from this gifted young racer. Thankfully, this young man, as well as others, continue to carry the Gospel to the tracks. I pray they are able to win more races than we ever did and reach more lives than we ever could.

This was only one of many creative ideas given to us by the Holy Spirit. I am careful to recognize His integral part in any success we had on or off the track. He truly deserves all the glory.

I've learned the importance of searching out creative ideas. As gifted as we may think we are, and as smart as we may want to believe we are, creative ideas are often the thing that sets us apart from our competition.

Creative ideas are often required to help us navigate through troubled waters and reach *the other side*.

It is important that we refuse to fear a changing paradigm or unique solution. It's important that we are willing to embrace change and accept new ideas and solutions that might provide the solution we need.

A different way of thinking may be just the thing that unlocks your destiny. Everything we take for granted today was once a creative idea that needed to be cultivated. Electricity, cars, airplanes, computers, the Internet, television, satellite TV, streaming TV, microwave ovens, etc., etc., etc.

> *Creative ideas are often required to help us navigate through troubled waters and reach the other side.*

As a child, I remember watching the Jetsons cartoon and thinking how cool it would be if we were able to make a video phone call. At the time, the necessary technology did not exist. Today, whether I'm across town or in another country, I make video phone calls on a routine basis. In fact, my grandchildren Graham and Hollyn, FaceTime me just about every night. I can only imagine how they might communicate with their grandchildren in fifty years.

How many creative ideas are still being withheld, simply because they have yet to be explored? Unlock the prison cell and free yourself from yesterday's way of thinking.

Living in the past is a dead-end road. The pathway to *the other side* requires a mentality that is fresh and current.

I've always found it interesting how we offer up motivational speeches about thinking outside the box and coloring outside the lines. Yet, when we teach our children to color, we correct them for that very thing.

If you ever hope to reach the other side, you will need to consider every option, every possibility, every virgin pathway, every creative idea. Your inability to recognize a solution is not indicative of the solution's existence. We've all heard the seven last words of a dying organization, *"We've never done it that way before."* This is true for your business, your church and your family.

I believe there are seeds of greatness, seeds of success, seeds of happiness all sleeping deep inside your being. It's time to wake them up and give them the life they crave. You may find that they wake you up in return, helping you find the creative solutions for everything you desire and deserve . . . on *the other side.*

Chapter 12

The Bottom Falls Out

Life had finally found some sense of normalcy for us. The church was healthy and growing. Business ideas were prospering. The racing ministry continued to excel. All the things we prayed for had seemingly opened up for us.

It seemed to be a perfect season for our family. We had our health. We finally had a few extra dollars in the bank. We had managed to string together several years of sanity in our marriage.

At last, we had turned the corner on all the problems of the past. We had made it out of the gutters of defeat and found our way back to the pinnacle of success.

Then one seemingly ordinary night, a dark ghostly figure, in the shape of a very large man, walked into our bedroom and stood at the end of our bed.

Tammye was asleep beside me. I hadn't fallen asleep just yet. I wasn't having a dream. My eyes were wide open as I watched this ominous figure walk right into our room and look me in the face. It was as if his eyes burned with fire, piercing directly to my soul. His haunting words were a message from a persistent enemy that had tormented us for many years. In a voice that wasn't audible, but yet was undeniably clear, he said these horrifying words.

"I will destroy your family, your ministry
and everything you hold dear.
It will all be taken from you."

I recognized this enemy. I recognized it as the demonic spirit that had attacked me on another occasion a few years earlier. That particular time, it came into my room and began to choke me. For several minutes I struggled to breathe. Thankfully, Tammye was with me on that occasion and prayed it away. I believe she saved my life that night.

> ❦
>
> *"I will destroy your family, your ministry and everything you hold dear. It will all be taken from you."*

This was the same demonic spirit that presented itself to me while on a trip to Moscow, threatening that I would never be allowed to return home to my family.

I was not afraid of this demonic spirit that decided to pay me another visit. It had no power and no authority over my life nor over my family. We were children of God and had all the power of heaven at our disposal. We understood our position of authority over the enemy.

We weren't afraid of this spirit nor of his assignment against us. We did, however; recognize this was no game. A demonic strategy had been put in motion to destroy us, and this time we would be in for the fight of our lives.

Ephesians 6:11 reminds us, *"Put on the full armor of God, so that you can take your stand against the devil's schemes."* One translation says, *"the strategies of the devil."*

Second Corinthians 2:11 encourages us not to be ignorant of Satan's devices, lest he gain advantage of us. Other translations say *"not to be ignorant of his schemes or strategies."* The Greek word used for *"ignorant"* in this verse literally means "to be without understanding."

> A demonic strategy had been put in motion to destroy us, and this time we would be in for the fight of our lives.

I am a firm believer that Christians have authority over the enemy, Satan and all his cohorts. I have had many years in the study of this truth. Likewise, I have spent more than thirty years teaching this revelation to others. Regardless, it would be up to us to put on the full armor of God and stand strong in the face of an evil attack. It would be paramount to have a clear understanding of the enemy's strategy and thwart it at every turn.

Many believers have mistakenly thought they were exempt from persecution, simply because they were believers. Quite the contrary, believers are more apt to be persecuted—because of their faith.

The Bible never promises a life without persecution and struggles. It does promise a way of victory through the storm. Psalm 23, one of the most notable and often quoted passages, says, *"Though I walk **through** the valley of the shadow of death."* I wish it said we would never have to walk through a valley, but it doesn't say that.

Unfortunately, society often passes judgment on those who walk through difficult circumstances—often believing they must have committed some horrible atrocity against God and humanity or they wouldn't be facing difficulties.

I think it's worth noting, some of the greatest leaders in the Bible faced immeasurable challenges. Many, for no other reason than because of their faith. Daniel faced a night with the lions. The three Hebrew boys faced the fiery furnace. Paul was imprisoned, shipwrecked, stoned, left for dead, chased out of numerous cities and persecuted in just about every way imaginable. All because of their faith.

Every attack against these great men was the direct result of a demonic assignment against them. Please understand, in no way, shape or form am I trying to imply that I am in the same league of spirituality with these men. I do contend, however, that each and every individual, especially believers, are squarely in the crosshairs of demonic strategies, schemes and plots directly from the pit of hell.

> *Each and every individual, especially believers, are squarely in the crosshairs of demonic strategies, schemes and plots directly from the pit of hell.*

Thankfully, God promised we could be victorious over EVERY demonic attack. His Word declares a *"greater"* power lives in us as believers. He declared that we have authority over every power of the enemy. It would be up to us to exercise that authority and stand firm in the victory we have been promised. For our family, this would prove more difficult than any battle we had ever faced.

As people of influence, carrying many gifts and talents, the enemy was even more intent to take us down. If so, it would be a great victory for the bad guys. Not to mention, if they could take us down in clear view of the public eye, appearing that our faith couldn't save us, it would have even greater significance. It was quite possible it would even discourage a few people along the way from walking in the faith we had so adamantly shared.

We were determined in our faith. We had been through hell and back before. We weren't afraid or discouraged. Disturbingly so, the events that transpired over the next few years would boggle my mind. In a million years, I would never have believed we would face a colossal attack of this magnitude.

The nightmare began in our marriage—a familiar place of attack. One would think we had overcome enough struggles in our marriage so that we could never be caught off guard again. I wish I could tell you this were true. It wasn't.

For reasons that are beyond the pages of this book, Tammye and I began to struggle. The long searched for happiness now seemed a million miles away. Things that once brought joy no longer sufficed. The bickering had returned. Snide, insensitive comments pursued invasive criticisms.

Suddenly, the cracks in our foundation had opened up like uncharted chasms of the deep.

We began to fight like never before. Innocent comments drew repulsive responses to otherwise harmless situations. The color of the sky argument had once again reared its ugly head. Apple pie had suddenly lost its satisfying appeal. The cool evening breeze now felt like a torrid flame ascending directly from the gates of hell.

Suddenly, the cracks in our foundation had opened up like uncharted chasms of the deep.

As we began to struggle more and more, our insensitivities started bleeding over into the church. This was understandable. After all, whatever resides on the inside of us will ultimately ooze out and touch those closest to us.

Slowly and surely, families began to leave the church. This meant their service and generous support were leaving as well. A once vibrant and thriving congregation was quickly becoming a shell of hopelessness.

In the midst of this turmoil, Tammye's job hit a dead end and she was forced to change career paths, taking a measurable decrease in salary. Suddenly, our little nest egg smelled less of a nest and more of a rotten yoke.

This was also around the same time the U.S. economy took its deepest plunge since the Great Depression. This too had a devastating effect on charitable contributions, thus deepening the strain on ministry finances.

Where was all this going? When would it end? Surely it couldn't get any worse. This was already enough to destroy most families I knew. I was deeply concerned. We wouldn't be able to withstand many more attacks.

In this midst of our dysfunction, Austin was attempting to navigate his senior year at school. It was supposed to be a time of fun and celebration. There was definitely no fun and beyond his graduation, very little to celebrate.

Yet today, we feel horribly responsible for our negative contributions to such an important season in his life. Without question, it left an indelible stain on the memory of his senior year.

> *For those in marriages who contend that their discontent will have a negligible effect on their children, you are grievously mistaken.*

For those in marriages who contend that their discontent will have a negligible effect on their children, you are grievously mistaken.

Sadly, and to our chagrin, things did get worse. Our fighting went from a small war to way beyond anything human. It was to the point we despised even being in the same room together. There were only two things

Tammye and I agreed on; we loved Austin and we held a considerable disdain for each other.

Things had gotten about as bad as they possibly could. There was little to be thankful for at Thanksgiving. The grinch had obviously stolen our Christmas. It felt like even God had stopped coming to our house.

Something had to change. Something had to give. Someone needed to move out. Who would it be?

We couldn't live under the same roof any longer.

Reluctantly, we decided that Tammye would be the one to move. She had some friends who would allow her to move into their empty house until it sold.

> *We couldn't live under the same roof any longer.*

I will never forget the pain of that week. It was my birthday week. Somberly, the three of us; Tammye, Austin and I went to lunch for my birthday. It was anything but a birthday celebration. Truthfully, we only went out of respect for Austin. It was for certain the worst birthday of my life.

At the very least, we thought we could put up the appearance of happiness. Austin was not fooled, nor was anyone else for that matter. This was not happiness. It was more like torture.

Tammye had already begun packing her things, preparing to move them to the other house. Sadly, all that was left was a sad and painful good-bye lurking in the depths of despondency.

Through every ugly word, every outburst of anger and disgust, one thing seemed to persevere just beneath the surface. *We still loved each other.* I know that may seem difficult to explain, but it's true.

We had loved each other deeply since our first date. Even though we knew this, we couldn't find the strength nor the understanding necessary to find peace in our home.

Deep inside, we were still hopeful we could find a resolution. It didn't seem likely in the near future, but anything's possible. For the time being, we decided it would be better to love each other from across town than to hate each other from across the room.

With that, we sat down in the floor, just outside our bedroom door. The same door that dark ghostly demon walked through only months before. We were crying so hard we could barely contain ourselves. Were we really going to do this? Is she really moving out? How did we ever get to this point?

As we sat in the floor crying, against all odds, we held hands and asked God to somehow help us. We were so far gone, we couldn't help ourselves. We were so confused and lost. *"Please, God, please . . . we just need help."*

> *Finally, the time came. During the season when we were supposed to be celebrating my birthday, she got in her car and drove away.*

Finally, the time came. During the season when we were supposed to be celebrating my birthday, she got in her car and drove away.

I don't know how Tammye dealt with the situation, but I cried for weeks after she left. It was useless trying to sleep. I had no appetite, no drive, no peace, no joy. Hopeless would have been a step in the right direction. More than ever before, I felt completely helpless. The despondent grasp of despair seemed to tighten with every breath.

Austin decided to make the move with Tammye. Even though I encouraged him to go with her and make sure he took care of his mother, it was incredibly difficult to watch both of them go.

Our once vibrant home was now empty and devoid of anything that left an aroma of peace. Where had it all gone? How could this have ever happened? Most of the time, the lights in the house remained off. It was almost as if you could smell the sense of loss and defeat.

A few days removed, I made the second hardest decision I had ever made. I went to the courthouse and filed for divorce. Partly out of anger. Partly out of pain and frustration. Confused and dejected, I filed the decree that merely acknowledged what everyone around us already knew—our marriage was in ruin.

I later met Tammye on the parking lot at Walmart and gave her the papers to sign. Somewhere deep inside, I suppose I secretly prayed she wouldn't sign them. To my surprise, I would later find out that she never signed. Surreptitiously, she too was praying for an answer.

Our lives were in shambles. Everything we had worked so hard for was gone. Our marriage was a mess. Our ministry stained. Our legacy impaired.

Just when we thought it couldn't get any worse, it did.

Amidst our discontent, my mother was diagnosed with a medical condition that would threaten her life. Simultaneously, my father was diagnosed with cancer.

Just when we thought it couldn't get any worse, it did.

This just wasn't fair. It was bad enough Tammye and I were living in two separate houses. Now the enemy has deployed attacks against my parents.

They had done nothing wrong. They were the most godly people I had ever been around. A familiar scripture suddenly became all too familiar, *"It rains on the just and the unjust."*[8] This was no ordinary rain. This was more akin to the deluge of Noah's time.

As if I was listening to a late night infomercial, the darkness seemed to spurn, *"But wait, that's not all."*

I couldn't take any more bad news. It was already more than any one family could deal with. What could possibly be next?

Apparently, the IRS decided this would be a good time for another audit of my tax returns. Not only would they audit three years of records, they would allege money laundering, fraud, tax evasion and a laundry list of other violations.

They systematically threatened to seize all of our accounts as well as any other accounts that may have my name attached to them. They threatened to take our house, plunder our list of contributors at the church and if I refused to cooperate, they were prepared to give me an all-expense paid vacation at the nearest 6 x 9 government housing project.

I knew we had done nothing wrong, but it would require thousands of dollars as well as the best attorneys and CPA's money could buy just to prove we were clean.

This was without question the darkest and most difficult season of my life. For the first time ever, I found myself questioning the faith I had so adamantly preached. The problems we had faced previously paled in comparison to the grief and hardships we were up against now.

This was not how our life was supposed to turn out. This was not the legacy we wanted to leave. This was not our destiny. We were winners. We were the good people—the ones who always found a way to win. This time darkness was daring to prove different.

We were in the depths of despair. Tammye and Austin had moved out. I had filed for a divorce from the love of my life. Mom and Dad were both facing deadly battles with very serious diseases. The IRS was exhibiting the incomprehensible abuse of its overreach and intimidation. The church was about to close its doors. Our finances were in total disarray. Debt was mounting faster and more fiercely than ever before. To top it all off, our friendships were drying up more quickly than morning dew in the desert.

I now knew how Jonah must have felt in the belly of that fish. The difference was, I didn't care to be spit up on the shore. I would've been just as satisfied to drown in the depths of the abyss. I was already in the depths. Drowning should've been the easy part. If nothing else, it might put me out of my misery.

Regrettably, I spent many nights contemplating how I might end my life. Death had presented itself as a viable option for relief. Deep down, I knew it was a terrible choice, but I wasn't thinking clearly. I wanted the pain and despair to stop, and I couldn't seem to find any way to alleviate the struggle. Night after night, I prayed that I wouldn't wake to see the morning.

To this day, I am sympathetic to those who find their way to the depths of this darkness. I wasn't a bad person and neither was Tammye. We just couldn't find our way out of the prison of futility we had come to know so intimately.

Likewise, not every person who struggles with depression, suicidal thoughts, anger, animosity, despair, divorce, addiction or any other form of torment should ever be written off as a person with no regard for quality of life. Quite possibly they are the result of an all-out assault by a demonic force assigned to destroy their faith and steal their soul.

The other side can often seem too distant for reach; beyond any conceivable path, impossible to gain, regardless of how strong the desire and how fierce the fight. This is without question one of the greatest lies the enemy levies on its target.

Never let the enemy convince you to give up and quit. It's as simple as that. NEVER GIVE UP!

When Jesus cautioned Peter about his certain denial, He said something very strange. Rather than encouraging Peter not to fail, Jesus reassured him, *"He was praying that his **faith** didn't fail."* This is monumentally important.

As we are often caught up in a person's failure, God is not. He is more concerned that their faith remains strong. He knows full well we are not capable of living a perfect life.

We make mistakes, then we make the same stupid mistake again and again. It is futile to think we can live our lives in perfection. It is just not possible. Yet, we offer that pressure to others, even ourselves, that we cannot allow failure to exist in our culture. The expectation of perfection in our daily lives is an open admonishment of our ignorance and our arrogance.

> *Never let the enemy convince you to give up and quit. It's as simple as that. NEVER GIVE UP!*

Don't get me wrong. I'm not advocating we have a license to sin. Obviously, we sin more than we ought without any license to do so. I'm advocating a pure heart and strong faith are more critical to our success than the presence of flawless living.

Regardless of our shortcomings, intended or accidental, God still loves us deeply. Regardless of how deep our despair may run, hope is only a breath away.

Don't allow the futility and frustration of your problems to rob you of the childlike faith that cries out from beneath your pain.

Refuse to give up! Refuse to allow the enemy to defeat you! Refuse to allow the cares of life to destroy the fiber of who you really are—God's child.

> *Don't allow the futility and frustration of your problems to rob you of the childlike faith that cries out from beneath your pain.*

It doesn't matter how bad the situation might seem. Set your sails into the wind and chart a course for *the other side* — a place of grace and peace.

Chapter 13

Help!
I've Been Shot!

I was raised around five sets of brothers, all about the same age. Some of my fondest memories as a child include these boys. We were always together, playing games, riding motorcycles, throwing rocks and just about anything else we could get into.

The father of two of the brothers was raised on a farm. He liked to gather up our band of brothers and take us fishing or hunting or swimming. Usually it was a combination of all three. We were out to have fun. It didn't matter where he took us or what we got into. We enjoyed being together and learning about life.

He told us stories of what it was like when he was our age. Stories that seemed bigger than life. I thought for sure he must have grown up with John Wayne. I had never heard stories like the ones he told.

He told us how his father would send him out to hunt for rabbits or squirrels. It was his job to bring something home for dinner, or else the family might not have anything to eat. His father would tell him how important it was that he not waste bullets, so he only gave him one bullet.

Can you believe that? First of all, to give your twelve-year-old son a gun, then tell him to go hunting by himself and then only give him one bullet. That's just crazy! Anyone with any smarts at all should know that's not right. You just can't do that with a twelve-year-old boy.

He's gonna need more than one bullet . . . right?

Well, I heard a lot of stories like this. Stories that still resonate in my mind today. I have many great memories of those days. I am forever grateful for the love and attention this man gave to us boys. Most Saturday mornings, his wife cooked a big breakfast and fed us before we took out for the day. It was never dull around that breakfast table. We laughed and talked about all the fun things we did the past week, and then we'd load up in his truck and take off on another adventure.

There's a rumor, I will neither confirm nor deny, about one of our little adventures. It was one of our usual Saturday rabbit hunting trips. Of course, it started with a big breakfast and lots of laughs, then we were off.

I believe I was somewhere around twelve or thirteen years old at the time. We were hunting rabbits out around some old coal mining strip pits. Before we took out after the rabbits, we first had to listen to his lecture about safety. After all, you don't give teenage boys guns and send 'em through the woods without a stern warning about potential dangers.

Sure, we had heard it all before, but we still stood there and listened. Never mind that it was cold. Never mind that the beagle hounds were bawlin' and bayin', ready to go to work and chase after those 'wascally 'wabbits. We stood there, though I'm not convinced we were listening.

The instructions began, *"Be careful where you walk. Be careful when you're crossing a creek or around the ponds. You don't want to fall in the water when it's this cold. Never run with a loaded gun. ALWAYS WATCH*

WHERE YOU'RE AIMING AND DON'T SHOOT EACH OTHER!!!
Don't chase after the dogs. The dogs will run the rabbit, usually in a big
circle and then right back to you. Just be patient and let the dogs do their
thing. Don't chase the dogs and **DON'T SHOOT EACH OTHER!"**

We knew it was important and the last thing we wanted was for someone to have an accident. *"God, help us to have fun, get lots of rabbits and no one get hurt."* That was the essence of the group prayer, and finally we were off.

We cut the dogs loose and the race was on. Right away, they were on a trail. Bawlin' and bayin', away they went. Their noses to the ground, tails in the air, lickety-split, they're gone.

Now, if you've never experienced this, it is a special moment. One that can't be put into words, just how euphoric it is. The blood starts pumping. Eyes wide open. *"I think I saw one!"* somebody yells. *"He's over here!"* The dogs start off on the chase as the furry little bunny runs for his life. Destiny awaits us all.

"Get ready! Get ready! He's coming your way! Get ready!" we yelled to each other.

It was a fury of activity that lasted for hours, sometimes all day. For us, it lasted until the dogs gave out or we ran out of bullets. Either way, it was game on and we loved it.

Rabbits were runnin', dogs were chasin' and us boys were giving it our best to see who could bag the most rabbits. It was high energy from start to finish. The saddest part of the day was when it was over.

Rabbits, dogs, boys. Rabbits, dogs, boys. Rabbits, dogs, boys. Get the picture?

As the chase ensued it happened, out of the trees and brush . . . ran that 'wascally 'wabbit. Immediately it was followed by a caravan of yelps and barks. The dogs were hot on his trail as fast as they could run. They were so close to catchin' him. Around the pond, across the creek, through a thicket. Those ole' hounds were just inches from catching that rabbit.

KAABOOOOM!!! A shot rang out. Suddenly . . . there was a squeal, a shriek, such an awful scream like I've never heard before.

"HELP! I'VE BEEN SHOT! I'VE BEEN SHOT!"

The scream cut through the morning fog like a hot knife through butter. *"Somebody, help me! I've been shot! Oh, God! I've been shot!"*

No, it wasn't the rabbit screaming. He was safe and sound, headed for the haven of a hole in the ground. The screams came from one of the guys hunting with us. He'd been shot! I will neither confirm nor deny exactly who it was that shot him. Needless to say, we were all very scared. Would he be okay? Was he bleeding? Was he going to die?

> *"HELP! I'VE BEEN SHOT! I'VE BEEN SHOT!"*

Wait just a minute. We noticed that the man who brought us hunting and gave us the safety speech was watching this whole episode unfold from his perch on the side of a small hill, just above the chaos. Why wasn't he running down to help? Why wasn't he screaming in a wild panic? Better yet, why was he laughing? Yes, laughing. He and his oldest son (one of my buddies) were about to fall into the pond, because they were laughing so hard. Well, folks, it wasn't funny to everyone, especially the guy who'd been shot.

Finally, the screaming and squealing came to an end. It had been replaced with a substantial amount of whining, moaning . . . and then, laughing. He wasn't hurt—not bad anyway. He was far enough away from the blast that the pellets from the small shotgun only left some very distinguishing whelps on his back. Thank God for several layers of thick clothing and for protecting us from an unforgettable tragedy. In the end it was unforgettable, but in an oddly humorous way.

"Okay, boys," the sermon part two began. *"Do you remember what we talked about? It is very, very important to watch where you're shooting. Guns are dangerous, and we absolutely don't want anyone getting hurt."* Then as he turned to the guy who got shot, the boy's dad said, *"I told you NOT TO CHASE THE DOGS!"* (By the way, the man who was shot was one of the grown men who was supposed to be teaching us boys how to hunt.)

To this day, I can't go rabbit hunting without remembering that story and those instructions. I still remember to not chase the dogs, and I am very careful where and what I shoot. For the record, I have never shot anyone else since that dreadfully humorous day.

*Gun safety is no laughing matter. Unfortunately, tragic accidents occur far too often. In no way, shape or form is it my intention to make light of the many situations in which children and adults are injured by misuse or mishandling of a dangerous weapon.

I do want to draw an analogy between the far and near. Metaphorically speaking, people are shot, and shot at, all too often. Whether we're the intended target of ill-advised activity or perhaps we are just in the wrong place at the wrong time, we feel the sting.

The Apostle Paul made reference to this when he spoke of the enemy shooting *"fiery darts"* at us. Some may want to dismiss the spiritual aspect that correlates with this story, but I can assure you it is very real.

Consider the immediate effect when you learned your best friend lied to you, or when you discovered your spouse cheated on you. Consider how you felt to learn your boss misled you on that promised promotion, only to find out someone else with less experience and less tenure was awarded the job. Or how did it feel the moment you received a call from the police, telling you they had arrested your son for drugs? Or when your fourteen-year-old daughter, the one on the superintendent's honor role, announced to you that she was pregnant?

The human language is completely inadequate to describe the pain and heartfelt disappointment of those moments. Some have described the feeling *"like I had been shot in the gut."* Excruciatingly painful. Hopelessness sinks deeper and deeper with each breath. Panic rings its bell loud and clear. Despair immediately kicks down the door and announces it has a new home.

Thankfully, I have never been shot (literally), but I have experienced pain and trauma in ways that I would equally describe, "I felt like I had been shot in the gut."

What now? What should I do? Where should I turn? This is absolutely the worst day of my life. I'm finished. My reputation is ruined. I'll never be able to get past this. I should run away and never come back. Maybe I should do something even more final.

Quite possibly these are some of the thoughts you experienced during that moment of disaster and demise. Equally so, this is all part of the enemy's plan to destroy you. The enemy doesn't care if you lose your job, your car or any of the other possessions that you deem valuable. ***The goal is to destroy YOU.***

Thankfully, getting shot or shot at isn't always fatal. In terms of the spiritual or emotional analogy, it is never fatal and never final. It may be a monumental setback, but it is survivable. It may cause considerable challenges and seemingly insurmountable obstacles, but I can assure you, it is possible to make it to *the other side.*

Chapter 14

Why Did God Do This to Me?

Job was a businessman in the Bible. According to scripture, he lost everything—his family, his wealth, even his friends. He too was the target of an all-out assault. The story of Job is still referenced today when someone loses everything.

Job was described as a man who was *"blameless and upright; he feared God and shunned evil."* We often make the mistake of thinking we are not candidates for tragedy as long as we do right, keep a good name in the community and go to church as often as possible. This couldn't be further from the truth.

You are the target of an invasive, malevolent strategy that transcends generations. Your good intentions will not deter it. Your family name will not discourage it. Your political connections will not alleviate it. Even your collection of lucky rabbit's feet and juju beads is not enough to eradicate the enemy's plan.

You may have heard the expression, *"It rains on the just and the unjust."* This actually is derived from the Bible verse in Matthew 5:45

where Jesus said the same sun shines on all people, the good and the bad. Likewise, the same rain falls on all people.

It's completely inaccurate to think we have some special immunity that keeps us from being targeted by the enemy.

When football teams practice, the quarterback typically wears a different color jersey, with explicit instructions to the other players, *"Do not hit the quarterback during practice!"* As much as I wish we could have that distinction in life, it simply isn't the case.

> ✎
>
> *It's completely inaccurate to think we have some special immunity that keeps us from being targeted by the enemy.*

Imagine walking down the street when it begins to rain. Oddly enough, not everyone is getting wet. Only the bad people are getting rained on. The nice people are dry. They don't even need an umbrella.

Imagine how life would be if nice people never had flat tires. They never faced health or financial challenges. Nothing bad ever happened to them, only good. Sadly, this is what some want to believe, but it just isn't so.

How is it that two people can look at the same picture, yet see a completely different image? How can two listen to the same song, yet hear something distinctly different? You've heard the expression, *"Is the glass half full or half empty?"*

Our perspective plays a monumental role in our experience.

More times than I can count, I've witnessed people facing tragedy and disappointment. Unfortunately, the person most often blamed for the problem is . . . **God**.

Why are we so driven to blame God for everything bad in our life, yet credit luck when something good happens? This ambivalent mentality is horribly flawed and brings perilous restrictions to our faith.

It is commonly accepted in most of our culture that God is some white-headed old man sitting on a cloud throwing lightning bolts at us any time we get out of line or say a bad word. It is also accepted that God is in *"complete and absolute"* control of everything that happens in our life. These illusions have been debated for generations and still cloud our way, even today.

> *Our perspective plays a monumental role in our experience.*

Listen to me, we are NOT robots. Life is not a video game, with God controlling every move. We are free moral agents. We have the legal right to make choices for our life. Right or wrong, we have the legal authority to make those choices.

What if we make the wrong choice? What if we slip up? What if we do something terrible and tragic that hurts others? What will happen? What will God do? What will He think of us? Listen close. *God is not an evil Creator waiting to strike us down when we slip and fall.*

I loved watching my grandson scurry around as he learned to walk. I asked his father, my son, **"Do you love him less when he falls?"** *"Of course not,"* he replied. *"If anything, **I love him more**, because I know it hurt when he fell."* Think about the power of that statement. How do you think our Heavenly Father feels about us when we fall?

Recently, a dear friend died in a traffic accident. The accident was caused when another driver "accidentally" pulled out into oncoming traffic. The tragedy affected an entire community. In the midst of grieving, a co-worker said to me, *"I'm just mad at God! I can't imagine why He would do this to our friend."*

"Wait a minute," I said. *"God didn't do this. This was an accident, pure and simple. Tragic for sure, but an accident."*

Why are you angry at God?

Years ago, I encountered a family facing a terrible tragedy. Three high school girls were riding in a pickup after school one day, having fun, just kids being kids. They were on the highway that ran through their rural community when they hit a semitruck head on. Two of the girls were killed instantly, the third was thrown through the windshield, onto the front of the semi, then dragged nearly 100 feet down the highway.

She was life-flighted to the nearest hospital where the doctors broke the news to her family. *"She's alive at the moment, but we don't expect her to live very long. It could be a few minutes or a few hours. We are only keeping her alive through medical and mechanical intervention, long enough to discuss the possibility of donating her organs. You need to say good-bye to your daughter. We can't save her."*

The family called me to the hospital to pray with them. I was a young man in Bible college, not equipped to handle a situation of this magnitude. I suppose they viewed me as a connection to God, and they were in need of all the help they could get.

It was humbling, to say the least. *"Help us, God,"* was the only prayer I knew to offer. I wasn't sure what to do nor how to help, other than to be there and console the family. I didn't know what to say. Then again, what can you say at a moment like that?

As I sat there in the hospital's little conference room with the family, a million thoughts ran through my mind. This young lady was sure to die any time. At the moment she was alive, but barely. She was so battered, she wasn't even recognizable. At the time, I had never seen someone in such a horrific condition.

Without question, this was one of those moments people describe as *"being shot in the gut."* The family was in shock. Disoriented and emotionally wrecked, hopelessness was thick in the air. There was an ominous presence looming, as if to say, *"I'm here to take the girl."*

What I heard next only added to the pain. The father looked at me and said, *"I know God did this, just like He did when I was young."* It was a delicate moment and I had no intention of debating theology, but I had to ask, *"Why do you feel that way?"*

The father began to tell of a tragic hunting accident that involved he and his brother when they were young.

He went on to elaborate that since that dreadful day, more than twenty years ago, he had blamed God for what happened with his brother. Day after day, year after year, for more than half of his life, he believed God caused the pain and tragedy that brought him such discontent and sorrow. Now, facing the eminent death of his daughter, God was squarely in the crosshairs of blame again.

Suddenly, something completely unexpected and totally off the wall happened. Deep inside, I heard these words, *"Tell him, if he will forgive God, his daughter will live."*

Are you kidding me? How on earth could I even consider making a statement like that, much less saying it to a man who's preparing to bury his child?

There was a restlessness rumbling deep inside of me. *"What if I say it and she dies? Then he will really hate God. Who would ever believe something so crazy? What if I tell him and she lives? Is it worth the risk? Is this the place to say it? Is this God telling me to say it, or is it a trick from the enemy trying to confuse me and make matters worse?"* Those thoughts and a trillion more ran through me in the blink of an eye.

After a significant amount of inner prayer and consideration, I decided I would say it. The immediate family was also in the little room and heard every word.

I said to the father, *"I feel like I'm supposed to tell you something. First of all, God did not do this to your daughter, and He did not cause the accident with your brother. You have been carrying this unforgiveness for too long. It's time to let it go. If you will stop blaming God for the tragedies that you believe He caused . . .. your daughter will live."*

Yes, it was a heavy moment. Some would describe the silence as deafening. At that instance, I felt like every eye in the room was looking at me, a young college kid who was either incredibly ignorant or undeniably arrogant. Honestly, I'm not sure which assessment was more accurate. Nonetheless, I said what I felt compelled to say. To this day, I truly believe God directed me to speak those words.

As the father looked at me with disbelief and discontent, he calmly said, *"You can't make deals like that. You don't make deals with God, especially for another person's life. What gives you the right to even think that way?"*

I humbly explained that I wasn't making a deal and neither was God. This tragedy, much like the accident with his brother, was the work of the enemy. Jesus said, *"The thief comes to steal, kill and destroy. I come to give you life, and life more abundantly."*[10]

"This is clearly the work of a devious satanic strategy to destroy your family." I explained, *"Bitterness, unfounded blame and unforgiveness are barriers that hinder the goodness of God from flowing in our lives."*

With tears streaming down our faces, the father opened up his heart to God, releasing a lifetime of torment and misdirected blame. It was as if someone opened the window and fresh air started flooding into the room. At that moment, the grim reaper was escorted out of the room and commanded to stand down. He did not have the legal authority to take that girl's life.

I left the hospital later that night and returned home. I still lived with my parents, so I told them about the accident and the status of the young lady. What I didn't tell them was about the conversation I had with the father. Honestly, I was still unsure what the outcome would be.

I didn't sleep much that night. Truthfully, I expected a phone call telling me the young girl had passed away.

Early the next morning, the phone rang. As I picked up the receiver, I confirmed my suspicions. It was the hospital. A thousand questions immediately raced through my mind. What were they about to tell me? Is she okay? Did she pass away?

I answered, cautiously, *"Hello?"* It was the family, but the news was different than expected. Their daughter was still alive. The doctors only gave her a very small chance of survival; but at the moment, she was alive.

With the doctor's update, some may have heard she had a 99 percent probability of dying. We heard she had a 1 percent chance of living. Once again, we were faced with the opportunity to see the glass half full or half empty. Actually, this wasn't even half and half, but we still chose to see the best in the situation.

After months in ICU, she was finally moved to a regular room, where eventually she was moved to rehab, then ultimately released to go home. The last I heard, she was living a normal life with a family of her own. God had miraculously intervened.

The enemy tried to destroy her, but God was there to give her life. The evil forces of hell had attacked this entire family. Thankfully, they made it to *the other side* as a beautiful young life was spared.

You must allow this truth to settle deep in your heart; God is a good God and He loves you dearly. He sent His Son to help you, not to hurt you.

Even in the tough times, God will give you courage and strength. Second Corinthians 12:10 declares, *"When I am weak, I am made strong"*[11] because of Christ's strength flowing through me.

The presence of a storm does not indicate the absence of God.

If we allow Him, God will take the most difficult circumstances in our lives and use them to our advantage. Romans 8:28 says, *"And we know that in all things God works for the good of those who love him. . . ."*[12]

> ✄
>
> *The presence of a storm does not indicate the absence of God.*

Whatever storm you're facing today, allow God to give you strength to work through it with patience and perseverance. While you're working through it, watch as He does something beautiful, just because He loves you.

Chapter 15

Don't Lose Faith

Consider the story of Job. There is a popular belief that he lost everything. In reality, he didn't lose "everything." He didn't lose his *faith*.

In fact, those closest to him vehemently admonished him to deny his faith. "If God truly cared about you, why would He do this to you?" they insisted. However, Job recognized that God was not his enemy, and faith in God was the only thing that would help him make it through this trial.

Jesus once told Peter, *"The enemy is after you and wants to cause you to fail. I'm praying for you that your **FAITH** doesn't fail."*[13]

Isn't that interesting. Jesus was sympathetic to the fact that Peter would fail, but He encouraged Peter not to let his **FAITH** fail. If we had the same foreknowledge of events, most of us would have adamantly insisted that Peter do everything in his power to prevent this looming failure.

In our minds, we often view failure as final. It most certainly is not. Failure is not what destroys us. Losing faith and giving up is.

Here are a few things to understand about failure:

1. It does not have the power to destroy you.

2. It is never final.

3. It is never eternal.

4. It doesn't stop the world from turning.

5. It doesn't knock God off His throne.

6. Regardless of how many times you fail, you **can** get back up again.

7. Most importantly, it won't cause God to stop loving you.

Failure is not your defining moment. It's not *who* you are. It's what you did. Who you are is completely different than any action you may or may not have taken.

> *In our minds, we often view failure as final. It most certainly is not. Failure is not what destroys us. Losing faith and giving up is.*

Solomon, a man of great wisdom, said, *"The godly may trip seven times, but they will get up again."*[14] The inference is not on how many times you fall, but that you get back up again.

So, you made a mistake, and maybe it was a big mistake that hurt others. It is not the end. Your life is not over. Your dreams are not dead.

Never let past failure deny you of future success.

Job refused to curse God and turn from his faith. Even in the depths of despair, he refused to give up. He knew that God had not, would not and could not give up on him.

It may be hard to imagine, especially when everything's going great, that you could ever question God's love for you. I've learned that everyone has a breaking point. It's that moment in your darkest night and your deepest despair, the moment you decide, "I just can't take any more."

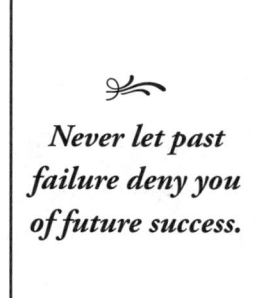

Never let past failure deny you of future success.

You begin to cycle through a long list of questions. "Why am I going through this? What did I do to cause this? Who can I trust? If God really loves me, why is He letting this go on? Why doesn't He step in and make everything better? If He's not going to help me, why do I need Him?"

I never imagined that I could reach that place. I was the one encouraging others. I was the one preaching hope and faith. That is, until I found my breaking point.

The enemy wants us to believe the pain will never stop, that the problem cannot be solved, that there is no solution and no way of escape. Before long we're convinced our pain will never end. It's been going on far too long, and it's not getting any better.

Most people don't stop to consider that Job's trial only lasted about nine months. In the end, Job received back twice as much as he had lost.

Peter failed miserably. He denied even knowing his best friend, Jesus. Think for a moment, how could our failures be any greater than what Peter did?

I love the way Jesus responded. When He arose from the grave, almost immediately He went to find Peter. When He found him, He simply asked, *"Peter, do you love Me?"*[15]

Jesus wasn't interested in talking about the failure. He wasn't caught up in being betrayed. He wanted to know that Peter's faith was still alive. Even if only a seed of faith, it would be enough.

Three times He asked Peter the same question, *"Do you love Me?"* It's important to note, three times Peter publicly denied Jesus, and three times Jesus publicly reaffirmed Peter. Each time Peter replied, *"Yes, I do love You."*

It's unfortunate, but true; people often hurt the ones they love the most.

Jesus' response was simple. *"Go feed my sheep."* He was essentially saying to Peter, "I'm not concerned with your failure. I'm looking at your heart. Don't let yesterday's mistake stop you from fulfilling your destiny. There is greatness inside you. Get up! Go to the other side of this failure, and let others be inspired by your courage. Pray for them, that their faith doesn't fail."

> ✱
> *It's unfortunate, but true; people often hurt the ones they love the most.*

I find it interesting that only a few days after his failure, Peter was preaching to thousands of people at the Festival of Pentecost. In most religious circles, Peter would have been banned for life, humiliated publicly and told that he would never see his destiny fulfilled. I'm so glad Peter wasn't subjected to the same religious hierarchy that so many hold dear today. He was held accountable to the law, but it was the law of liberty.

The law of liberty is actually a much higher standard than most realize. Rather than demanding compliance by letter of the law, it receives conformity by an endless degree of love.

I'm not married simply because I signed a marriage license and filed it at the courthouse. My marriage is based on a much higher system, a contract of love.

Imagine for a moment that you've committed a horrific sin. Rather than being ridiculed and cast out of your community, you were asked one simple question, "Do you love God?"

> *Your faith will build a bridge capable of carrying you across any divide.*

Your faith will build a bridge capable of carrying you across any divide. Never lose your faith. It is the wind in your sails. The peace in your storm. It is the one single thing above all else that you must protect.

Do not let your faith fail! It is the life-sustaining force that will insure your passage to *the other side*.

Chapter 16

I Didn't Know Cows Could Swim

Remember those boys I hung out with when I was younger? Well, this time it was warm weather and time for our band of brothers to do some fishing and swimming.

After trying our best angler skills at a handful of farm ponds, we decided to go for a swim in a small lake close to where we had been fishing. The same man who had often loaded us up and taken us on our Saturday journeys was leading the way again.

It was a small lake nestled away in the lush green hills of Northeastern Oklahoma. It was summertime and a perfect day for a bunch of smelly, dirty boys to cool down and have some fun in the water.

Once again, we had to stand by for the safety speech. The last thing we wanted was for someone to get hurt. It may sound harmless for boys to go fishing and swimming, but I know for a fact that it can be determinately hazardous. After all, I may or may not have accidentally hooked one of the boys in the face with an errant cast of my favorite fishing lure. (Of course, I will neither confirm nor deny that it was me, except to say I was there.)

We arrived at the lake, listened to the all-important safety speech and then it was time to do what boys do—have fun. We swam out a short distance to a small swimming dock, a few yards from the shore. It was a great place for boys to spend a summer day. Laughing, giggling, and pushing one another off the dock, only to find recompense in the favor returned. The games ensued. Anything we could think of to pass the day and show who was the fastest, strongest, bravest and craziest.

We had devised a game where we would throw an object from the dock, and then see who could be the first one to swim out and get it. Farther and farther we'd throw things. Faster and faster we'd swim out, then just barely get back to the dock before we gave out. Being the runt, I just couldn't seem to swim as far as the other boys. (I could obviously shoot straight and wheel a wicked fishin' pole. I just couldn't swim very far.)

That was the day I heard another story that would stick with me like peanut butter sticks to jelly.

My friend's father, who was raised around that very area, told one of the most improbable stories I had ever heard. I sat in amazement as I held on to every word. It was better than Batman and Robin saving Gotham.

He told us of a time when he was about our age, a young teenager growing up on the farm. The animals on the farm were his best companions. His world champion rabbit dogs, chickens that laid golden eggs, cows that gave the sweetest milk and his horse that was faster than greased lightning. In those days, a boy and his horse were inseparable; and if your horse was fast, you were on top of the world.

As we sat on the edge of that swimming dock listening to his stories, he said, "Boys, do you see that hill over there?" Almost in unison,

March 5, 1988

July 1991
Dave holding Austin in NICU

May 1993

1994
During our Oklahoma City years.

Christmas 1994
Tammye, her father,
Tom and her mother,
Patricia, 8 months
before she passed.

2009
Our best attempt to smile
through the pain.

Father's Day 1999
Tammye, Austin and her dad – just six
months before his sudden passing.

1972
My mom, brother and I.

November 2015
Preparing to open a new
company – Premier USA

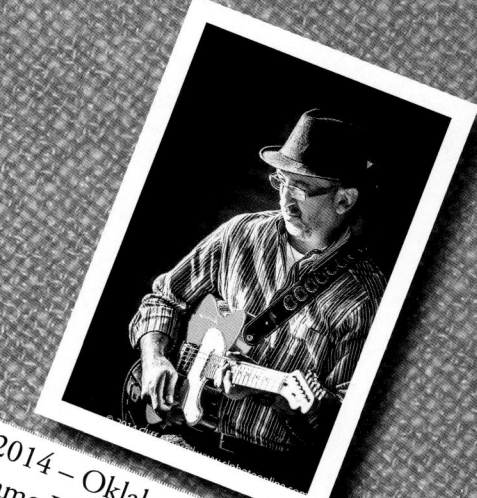

2014 – Oklahoma Music Hall of
Fame Playing guitar for a concert
with Jermaine Mondaine

2015 Date Night

2009 Racing Season

March 2013
Our 25th Wedding Anniversary

New Year's 2016
Niagra Falls, NY

2016
Valentine's Day

Puerta Vallarta, Mexico 2016
Project Dream Seeds Outreach

2016
Easter – Dave, his father, Carroll, his
mother Betty & his brother, Jeff.

Christmas 2017
Central Park, NY

Thanksgiving 2017
Austin & family

Christmas 2017
Dave, Tammye, with
Dave's mom and dad

2016
Dave at a village in
Quimixto, Mexico with
Project Dream Seeds

Christmas 2017
Central Park, NY

October 2018
St. Thomas, USVI

Oklahoma Music Hall of
Fame Induction
Ceremony 2018
That year we were the
hosts and MC's.

March 2018
Walking on Grace Beach
in Turks & Caicos
Celebrating our
30th wedding anniversary.

October 2018
St. Thomas, USVI

February 2019
Praying at a marriage
conference which we
hosted and helped direct.

May 2019 in
Destin, FL

May 2019 in Destin, FL
Dave, Tammye, our son Austin,
wife Kaitlyn and their children,
Graham & Hollyn.

Spring 2019
In front of
our new dream home.

2011

Walking across a foot bridge in the mountains above Puerto Vallarta, Mexico. We declared this bridge as "our bridge" signifying a walk to the other side. We travelled to this bridge on many occasion, just to remind ourselves of the other side.

we chimed, "Do you mean the one on the other side of the lake?" He said, "Ya, that's the one."

"When I was about your age, I came down to this very spot on my horse one day. I could swim really well, so I decided to try and swim across this lake to the other side."

Our eyes were wide open now. That seemed like such a long distance. Too far for anyone in our gang. "What happened?" we asked. "Did you make it?"

"Well, of course I made it, boys. I'm here today, aint' I?"

He went on to tell us how he used to swim across that lake all the time. That seemed so incredible to hear, especially for a bunch of strong teenage boys who could barely swim out a hundred feet or so to fetch a stick in a game.

It still amazes me, the things people can do when they're prepared or challenged. Sadly, it's often during the bad times that we find out just what we're made of and how strong we really are. So many things we would ordinarily never think of doing, we find ourselves doing in difficult times. Later, we look back and question how we ever made it through.

> *It still amazes me, the things people can do when they're prepared or challenged. Sadly, it's often during the bad times that we find out just what we're made of and how strong we really are.*

He went on to tell us that after he swam across the lake and back . . . He decided to see if he could swim his horse across. "Are you kidding me?" I thought. "That's absolutely ridiculous."

Sure enough, that's exactly what he did. He swam his best friend and equine extraordinaire across that lake to *the other side*, and back. Now I knew he must have grown up with John Wayne (or Batman).

You should've seen the look on our faces as we sat there on that swimming dock looking out across the lake. This was totally absurd. Not only did he swim across, but also swam his horse across. I didn't know what to think about this story. Suddenly, my mind was the one doing all the swimming.

Could it be that our truest companions in friendship are often right beside us when we navigate the currents of life? I'm sure his horse had other things in mind when he left the barn. What thoughts were going through his mind when his bareback jockey mounted up and pointed his nose toward the deep? It was one friendship that was about to be challenged.

I'm both thankful and regretful for the times that I've taken my friends and family on a dangerous journey into the deep waters of uncertainty. Trust rises to a new level after you've taken on the darkness. Win or lose, life is different beyond that defiant plunge. You are never the same again. In some ways, fear changes to confidence and you begin to believe you can do anything. In other ways, you decide to never go near the water again.

> *Trust rises to a new level after you've taken on the darkness. Win or lose, life is different beyond that defiant plunge.*

Then, the story became even more interesting. Since he knew that he could swim across; and now knew that his horse could swim across albeit rather reluctantly, it was time for the real test.

Remember that old milk cow with the sweetest milk? Well, hold on to your butter. The water's about to get really deep.

He actually tried to swim that old cow across the lake. That's both crazy and funny. Who sits around and thinks of doing something like that? I guess, if you're a teenage boy, raised on a farm in rural Oklahoma, anything's in play.

I can still remember what I was thinking while he was telling this story. *"I didn't know cows could swim,"* rambled through my mind again and again and again. It was hilarious, but then, it wasn't funny at all. As it turns out, that old cow wasn't quite the swimmer the horse had come to be. No, that old milk cow preferred to drink the water with her feet firmly in the mud.

"What happened next?" we prodded. "Did the cow make it? What did you do?"

"Oh, well . . . uh . . . no . . . Actually, the cow couldn't quite make it across," he laughed. However, he was able to get the cow back to shore before the Bismark sank.

Now the story had really turned funny. We were laughing so hard we nearly fell off that dock into the lake. Imagine that, trying to swim a big fat cow across the lake. Now that's funny! Even if you're not from around here, that's still funny.

Did you know cows could swim? Well, now you do as I myself learned that day on the dock.

There are many things about life we may not know. It doesn't mean they aren't true, simply because we didn't know it. In fact, there are many things about ourselves we may not know. The truth is, it may be the oddest and most unbelievable circumstances that help us learn who we really are.

Some of the most trying times in my life have been the most educational. I've always said, "The school of life is an effective teacher."

Pause for a moment and consider some of the difficult seas you've had to navigate. Did you learn anything? Were you wiser and smarter after the fact? It may be that you learned what not to do, but I'm sure you learned something.

It is often these real-life experiences that help shape us into the people we are. Think about it. You understand the power of healing, partly because you were sick. You appreciate the value of a dollar, because you've been without. You understand companionship, because you've also been alone.

> *It is often these real-life experiences that help shape us into the people we are.*

Don't underestimate the importance of your experiences. It may have been the darkest night of your life, but you survived to see the sunrise. It may have been the thickest fog, but you found clarity. The calamity of horrors may have even been a result of your own bad decisions. Still, you learned priceless truths.

Today, you also learned something. Cows can swim . . . just not as good as horses.

Chapter 17

A Fresh Perspective

Pay close attention. This is the moment when difficult decisions become even harder. This is the do or die, the stay or run, the make it or move on moment. This moment may very well determine whether or not you reach *the other side*.

It's quite possible you have identified with something in our story that relates to you. The names and dates are surely different, but the underlying belly of the situation may have many similarities.

This is where you need to turn off your cell phone and stop answering calls from all the people in your life who think they know what's best for you. Chances are, they have no clue.

This moment may very well determine whether or not you reach the other side.

It has always intrigued me why people would take advice from someone who has no solid foundation from which to advise. For instance, why take financial advice from someone who is always broke? Why take medical advice from someone who is always sick? Why take marital advice from someone who has been married nineteen times?

Holiday Inn Express has a brilliant advertising campaign that speaks to this very matter. They portray people giving critical advice in delicate situations. When asked if they're an expert and therefore qualified to give such advice, they reply, "No, but I did stay at a Holiday Inn Express last night."

We need to be very careful who we take advice from. This is not a car, or computer, or a coed softball game at the company picnic. This is our life! This is the future of our family. This may be the most important decision we've ever made. The legacy of our life is about to be revealed.

You can glean healthy insight from any situation. Your best information might even be what *not* to do.

In our case, we decided to go outside of our normal network and seek counsel from professionals who were specially trained and equipped with the necessary tools to help resolve the type of conflict we were facing. In this, we would end up visiting with multiple counselors until we found someone with whom we both felt comfortable and were able to relate to their anecdotes. Essentially, we found someone we trusted enough to put our lives in their hands. This was not an easy choice and did not happen overnight.

> *You can glean healthy insight from any situation. Your best information might even be what not to do.*

Notice, I did not say, "Someone we thought would give us the answers we wanted to hear." Turn your phone back on and ask your friends for that kind of advice. If you really want worthless advice, get on social media and let the whole world offer their comments. (This is not the time to air your dirty laundry on social media. STOP IT NOW!)

One area that continues to infuriate me is how people will take their car to the best mechanic they can find and pay a premium price to have it fixed. All because they value their vehicle. They'll search for the best doctor. One who has the expertise and experience to treat their problem with the greatest care. If necessary, they'll even sell all their possessions to raise enough money to pay for the treatment. After all, they only have one body and they need to keep it as healthy as possible.

Why then is it so difficult for us to seek out the best counselors and pay whatever is necessary to help resolve conflict in our family? Why is it so difficult to buy and read substantive material that will help alleviate the pain in our relationship? Why do we struggle to set aside quality time to go to counseling? Please, tell me why?

If you needed brain surgery, you wouldn't go to the mall and ask for someone who sold shoes. You wouldn't go to the hardware store and ask for someone who knew about hammers. You wouldn't go to the computer store and ask for the I.T. guy.

> *Why is it so difficult to buy and read substantive material that will help alleviate the pain in our relationship?*

This is your family, your marriage, your children. They should be the most important people in your life, next to God. Make an investment consistent with their value. Take the time. Spend the money. Invest in finding a solution.

Maybe the first investment should be to ask for help—for *you.*

As bad as things were for Tammye and me, we recognized that we needed help; not only for our marriage, but for ourselves, individually. Cautiously, we each agreed to go get help.

Over the next year or so, we spent countless hours and thousands of dollars searching for answers to our greatest dilemma. On numerous occasions, we had no money to pay for the counseling, so we used a credit card and charged it. This may not work for some, but we felt it was important. We considered the fact that we had financed TV's, furniture, tires for the car, dinner and other matters of life's routine. Isn't this a bit more important than any of those things?

> *Maybe the first investment should be to ask for help—for you.*

We didn't see each other every day, but usually found a reason to call or make some kind of contact. Strangely enough, I'm convinced there were times we made contact just to start an argument. It sounds weird, but we truly loved each other and wanted to be together. We simply couldn't find a way to be together without arguing over something. To make matters worse, the argument was typically over something that had absolutely no bearing or significance.

I've witnessed this in other families over the years. Almost like little puppies who needed the interaction of the other puppies, even when they were wrestling and fighting over a toy. It looked violent, but really it was harmless play.

For some, like us, it was not harmless and it was anything but play. It revealed a level of maturity, or should I say *"immaturity."* As tragic as it may sound, this is where many relationships struggle. They have never learned how to communicate with each other on a mature level.

To be clear, maturity and age do not always go hand in hand. More than I care to admit, there have been times when I acted extremely immature, even though I was well into my adult years. Childishly pathetic is a good way to describe it.

For Tammye and me, we were acting like a couple of five year olds fighting over a toy. Hopefully, you've never acted that way.

The childish and immature things we said and did during this dark time are horribly embarrassing, even today. We were an embarrassment to our family, our church, our friends and anyone else who had the unenviable task of being within a hundred miles of us.

> *To be clear, maturity and age do not always go hand in hand.*

Of the many things we knew we had to change, one was our perspective—the way we saw things. The way we looked at each other. The way we looked at our situation. The way we looked at any possibility we had at a future together and also, the way we looked at our past.

Perspective is critical, especially when trying to resolve conflict. It's not only what you see, but how you see it.

The optimist sees the glass half full, while the pessimist sees it half empty. One sees the mountain as an obstacle, while another sees it as an opportunity. One sees a career change as a step back. Yet, another sees it as a step up.

Perspective is important. It may be the difference between sickness and health, poverty and abundance or even life and death.

Advertisers spend billions of dollars trying to influence our perspective. Politicians spin every story to try and sway our perspective. Great leaders understand the importance of seeing and portraying the right perspective.

Sadly, for Tammye and me, our perspective was skewed and tainted. Muddled with our childish and selfish opinions of what we wanted and what we felt we deserved.

As our perspective began to change, we learned that everything wasn't as we had thought and certainly not as we had believed. We learned we had to be very cautious about who we listened to and what influences we allowed into our lives.

> ❧
>
> *Perspective is critical, especially when trying to resolve conflict. It's not only what you see, but how you see it.*

Simply because someone said they cared about us was no guarantee they actually did. Simply because they were once our friend offered no assurance they should continue to be. Relationships, co-workers, neighbors, friends and even a few family members, all needed considerable vetting to help ensure they really had our best interests at heart.

Consider the lasting effect of how one person's influence can affect the perspective of others. Eve was convinced, by one voice, to change her perspective on the forbidden fruit. Samson was seduced by one, Delilah, to change his perspective on who he could trust.

Who is in your life trying to persuade you to change your perspective? What voice is speaking to you about who you can or should trust? Before making a life-altering decision, you need to consider your perspective and who or what is influencing you.

Popular opinion can also be an overwhelming voice, especially when it speaks loud and often. Inaccurate views and strategies are often sewn into the fabric of a society by the persuasive voice of unhealthy contingents. Crowds get worked into a frenzy, when the otherwise calm and rational voices get carried away with a particular perspective.

Regardless of its authenticity, if the perspective is believed, it is perceived as apparent truth. It's been said, "My perspective is my reality."

Moses sent twelve spies into Canaan to spy out the land. Only two returned with a positive perspective. Because of the influence of ten men and the relative disobedience that followed, an entire nation suffered.

Peer pressure remains one of the most challenging influences on our perspective. Its influence can be overwhelming.

We need to surround ourselves with the right people. People who have the right perspective. Their influence on our perspective may be a critical piece in the puzzle.

Culture, history and social bias are also powerful influences on our perspective. We need to be very careful how we allow these areas to influence us.

Though Tammye and I continued to struggle, still living in separate houses, we made time to seek help, both as a couple and as individuals. We knew we could never restore our marriage and have a happy life together as long as we were unhealthy individuals. I'm not referring to our physical health, rather our internal health—spiritually, emotionally and psychologically.

If we could find a way to fix ourselves, it just might be possible to fix our marriage.

We continued to seek help, even though on many occasions, we drove separately to our counseling appointments. We struggled through the sessions grasping for answers and the appropriate response, searching for a better understanding of why and how we ever got to this place. It was awkward, embarrassing, humiliating and frustrating. Needless to say, it was extremely difficult.

> *If we could find a way to fix ourselves, it just might be possible to fix our marriage.*

155

As painful as it might have been, we hoped it would bring us to a better place in life. If we truly wanted to make it to *the other side*, we had to see the value in getting help.

After many of our counseling sessions, we would go to dinner or for a snack. Not to continue the session, rather to try and spend a few minutes together without fighting. There were rules we tried to adhere to: no rude comments, no fighting, no discussing our problems. We needed to just sit down together for a few minutes and try to enjoy a peaceful moment. That was quite challenging at times, but it was worth the effort.

Eventually, we started following some of the advice from our lead counselor. One such direction: instead of fighting over issues every day, or every time we spoke, we were encouraged to set a particular time each week when we would talk about whatever problem we wanted to discuss.

> *We learned how to be patient and that it was okay to talk about something other than problems, even if we still had problems. This would help us find our identity in something other than our conflict.*

This wasn't easy, especially if our next agreed upon talk was several days away. We learned to make a list and brought the list to the meeting. We discovered, by the time our little meeting rolled around, most of the things on the list were no longer relevant.

That was a great tool. It taught us, among other things, how to prioritize. We learned how to be patient and that it was okay to talk about something other than problems, even if we still had problems. This would help us find our identity in something other than our conflict.

This is a good piece of advice for pastors and business leaders to learn. We shouldn't bring all our problems home to our family. When we do have an opportunity to spend quality time with our family, we don't want to waste it talking about problems.

I realize we need to be able to communicate with our spouse and peers about the challenges we're facing, but we don't want to spend all our time talking about problems. Instead, we need to talk about how nice the weather is, or how pretty the birds are singing. Find something positive and healthy to talk about.

If we're not careful, our spouse may get tired of listening to all the problems. This often leads to extramarital relationships in an effort to replace the companionship that is lost in all the negative talk about problems.

There's a fine line that needs to be maintained, a balance of sorts. With this in mind, if we are not allowed to discuss any issues with our spouse, we may opt for a relationship outside of our marriage, looking for someone who will listen. This is also very dangerous.

In short, we need to talk to our spouse, but know when and what to talk about. In doing so, it is essential we establish and maintain healthy boundaries.

Another creative idea from our lead counselor also required a unique perspective.

Instead of divorcing each other, we divorced our broken marriage.

This was a completely new concept to us. Perhaps it's been around for generations, but it was an unfamiliar term for us.

The idea was a simple matter of perspective. "You love each other, but you hate what your marriage has become. Rather than divorcing each other, divorce your broken marriage. Start fresh from this point and build the relationship and subsequent marriage you desire, together."

It was a stretch, but it just might work. It couldn't make things any worse than they were. We were already living in two separate houses, fighting about anything and everything. If this didn't work, what more could we lose?

> *Instead of divorcing each other, we divorced our broken marriage.*

Above all else, we recognized our need for a new perspective. We had no intention of going back to the way things were. It didn't work in the past and wouldn't work in the future.

If our marriage was ever going to be anything worthwhile, we needed a new vantage point. If we had any hopes of reaching *the other side* of this perilous expanse, we needed to find an outlook that resounded of the peace we hadn't been able to fully embrace.

Our perspective was definitely changing. Hopefully it was changing in the right way. Hopefully we were getting a different glimpse of our life, one that was more accurate. Hopefully a new viewpoint would help get us where we wanted to go, *the other side.*

Chapter 18

Unconditional Love

That season of our lives was obviously a tremendous challenge to navigate. There were no easy days. Every day was a struggle, some more than others.

We were constantly searching for answers, creative solutions or an innovative idea that would somehow release us from this snare and magically deliver us to Dorothy's family farm in Kansas. We were eager to find something, or should I say, anything that would help.

In the midst of a constant search for answers and relentless prayers for peace, I heard something. It was that still small voice whispering gently to my spirit man. Words I hadn't expected. It was a strategy I wasn't sure I was ready to embrace. Nonetheless, I believe God visited me with an answer to my prayers. Surely, I needed to give it my undivided attention; regardless of how I felt about it.

As we often do, I too found it easy to lay all the blame on someone else. In my eyes, it was all Tammye's fault. I wanted to believe I had nothing to do with our problems. I convinced myself that I was the victim, not complicit in any way. I somehow forgot the demonic visit that promised to destroy us. I systematically placed the onus squarely on Tammye.

Obviously, my decisions and actions also played a role in our dysfunction. For various reasons, I chose to limit my responsibility, hoping my "super-Christian" persona would remain intact. Christian, huh? Well, in that case, I probably needed to follow the tenants of faith as outlined in the Bible. That was easier said than done, especially considering the words God was speaking to me. Softly and gently, He deposited these words deep in my spirit.

"Unconditional love."

"Love her unconditionally," He whispered to me. "Love her without expecting anything in return. Love her without bitterness. Love her without complications from the past or from her mistakes. Love her without a self-righteous ego. Love her without any regard for her actions or reactions whether past, present or future. Just love her . . . unconditionally."

> ❧
> *"Unconditional love."*

It was more than I was prepared to accept. More than I expected to be required of me. More than I considered fair. Perhaps even more than I thought was humanly possible.

As I pondered His words and challenge, I realized that many areas of our Christian walk, frankly most, if not all, have some kind of condition that accompany them. Even salvation is conditional in that we must call on God and confess Jesus Christ as our Lord and Savior. Love, however, is to have no conditions.

As I considered the challenge before me I wondered if it was more than I could do. I wanted to restore our relationship. I wanted to rebuild our family. I wanted to be a better husband and father. Let's be honest, though. Through it all there had been some ugly words and situations thrown at me. Of course, I then felt obliged to throw right back.

Believing the word came from God, I began to search the scriptures. What did the Bible say about love? How did it define unconditional love? What were the parameters? How far did I really have to go with this?

I immediately turned to a passage often referred to as the "love" chapter, 1 Corinthians 13. It's very common for this chapter to be read at weddings. It was given as a biblical definition of love. I knew this chapter. I had preached from this text many times. I had heard it at weddings more times than I could count. But I wasn't prepared for it to speak to me the way it did on that day.

THE NIV renders verses 4-8 in this way:

4 Love is patient, love is kind. It does not envy, it does not boast, it is not proud. 5 It is not rude, it is not self-seeking, it is not easily angered, it keeps no record of wrongs. 6 Love does not delight in evil but rejoices with the truth. 7 It always protects, always trusts, always hopes, always perseveres.

8 Love never fails . . .

Okay, that's not so bad. That's exactly the way I remembered it. Then I turned to the *Amplified Bible* and retrieved its translation. It was vastly more revealing.

Beginning at the end of the twelfth chapter, this is what I found.

31 But earnestly desire and zealously cultivate the greatest and best gifts and graces (the higher gifts and the choicest graces). And yet I will show you a still more excellent way [one that is better by far and the highest of them all—love].[16]

4 Love endures long and is patient and kind; love never is envious nor boils over with jealousy, is not boastful or vainglorious, does not display itself haughtily. 5 It is not conceited (arrogant and inflated with pride); it is not rude (unmannerly) and does not act unbecomingly. Love (God's love in us) does not insist on its own rights or its own way, for it is not self-seeking; it is not touchy or fretful or resentful; it takes no account of the evil done to it [it pays no attention to a suffered wrong]. 6 It does not rejoice at injustice and unrighteousness, but rejoices when right and truth prevail. 7 Love bears up under anything and everything that comes, is ever ready to believe the best of every person, its hopes are fadeless under all circumstances, and it endures everything [without weakening]. 8 Love never fails [never fades out or becomes obsolete or comes to an end] . . .

13 And so faith, hope, and love abide . . . .. love—[true affection for God and man, growing out of God's love for and in us], these three; but the greatest of these is love.[17]

1 EAGERLY PURSUE and seek to acquire [this] love [make it your aim, your great quest][18]

Ouch! That's not what I wanted to hear. The verse that stood out the most was the latter part of verse 5, *"It takes no account of the evil done to it [it pays no attention to a suffered wrong]."*

To be completely honest, I, like most people, had made a habit of keeping notes. I had recorded all the times I felt Tammye had done or said something that I didn't like. Not so much in a physical notebook, but in my mind.

Isn't that the way we typically react? We are very good at keeping score of the other person's flaws, but are quick to expect them to forget ours. It's the first thing we usually throw out when we get in an argument. "But you said . . . ! And you did . . . ! I remember the last time you . . . !"

It's no wonder we have such a difficult time resolving conflict in our relationships. Instead of searching for ways to forgive, love and move forward, we're still dragging up every old skeleton bone we can find.

It doesn't matter if it happened yesterday or fifteen years ago, too often we're eager to bring up past wrongs and expect some sense of accountability. We crave an offering from the depths of their soul promising a proportionate sacrifice, commensurate to the crucifixion.

However, when it comes to our own faults we tend to excuse them away saying, "By the way, I was just having a bad day and didn't really mean to say all those ugly things that came out of my mouth, so you can forget all about that."

Does this sound about right? Does it sound remotely familiar? I'll tell you what it does *not* sound like. It does not sound like unconditional love.

There seems to be a part of us that wants to keep record. In some twisted way, it allows us to feel superior and gives us a perceived position of power. This is completely and totally contradictory to the definition of love and beyond comparison to the definition of unconditional love.

I'll admit, I was having a problem with it—a big problem.

I feel I can take the liberty to make this next statement, primarily because I've served in full-time ministry for more than thirty years. I've served as pastor most of that time, and have been recognized with prophetic and apostolic gifts on my life. Likewise, I have a firsthand, intimate view of thousands of colleagues who also serve in the ministry. With that qualification, this is my observation . . .

Many who serve in high ministry offices struggle with a condition often referred to as "the God complex."

There is a perceived orientation that says, "Because I am in a position of authority, with the responsibility to teach others how they should live, I am also in a position to judge them. In the same light, I have the right to call them out on their shortcomings, regardless of how I might have also failed in the same or similar area. I am better than everyone else, simply because of the vocation into which I have been called."

Many who serve in high ministry offices struggle with a condition often referred to as "the God complex."

It grieves me to say, I was the chiefest of offenders. This weakness has roots that connect back to my old cell mate—pride. All of a sudden, I felt my wings melting again.

Tammye once had a dog named Doug. He was rescued from an abusive environment. We believe he was a mix between Terrier and Pit Bull. Thus, he had the hyper personality of a Terrier, with the body and strength of a Pit Bull. He and Tammye were best of friends. They went everywhere together, including the local drive-in where she would treat him to his own hotdog and fries.

Doug was extremely protective of her. He wouldn't even let me give her a hug or kiss without trying to protect her from me. If he had it his way, no one would ever get close to her.

Isn't it interesting that our favorite furry friends are often better examples of unconditional love than are we. Think about it. Regardless of how we treat our dog, he's still there waiting on us at the end of a long day, smilin', waggin' his tail and ready to play.

Amazingly, our pets quickly forget all about how we failed to feed them or give them fresh water. They let go of the fact that we tried to beat them for eating our favorite pair of shoes. They don't hold a grudge nor conjure up ways to get back at us. They aren't organizing all their tail-waggin' friends to attack us at first light.

They simply offer love. In fact, unless they are specially trained for a particular service or activity, most likely our pets have only two God-given purposes in life: to protect us and to love us—unconditionally. They would instantly, without hesitation, give their life to protect ours. That's somewhat enviable. That's true companionship. That's unconditional love.

Suddenly, I remembered the biblical charge given to men how we are to be willing to lay down our life for our wife, just as Christ laid down His life for the Church, all because of unconditional love.

Never again would I be able to hear those words, nor read that passage in Corinthians without a thunderous reverberation of conviction rising from deep in my soul.

I had to change.

I had to find a way to let go of everything which I had not yet released.

If we were going to have any chance of making it to *the other side*, I would have to learn how to love unconditionally. Regardless of anything Tammye did or didn't do, this was my first charge. I had to take responsibility for my actions. I wasn't her savior nor her judge. I wasn't her heart monitor, weighing her thoughts against my view of right and wrong.

I had been trapped in a perilous delusion. I had played right into the enemy's hand. I had made it easy for the enemy to destroy my family. I had to break free of the chains that bound me.

> *I had to change.*

Regardless of what Tammye decided to do or where she decided to go, I had to deal with the face in my mirror. How could I ever help her if I wasn't also willing to get help for myself? How could I ask her to love me unconditionally unless I was first ready to love her in the same way?

I accepted we might never put our family back together. We might never rebuild our marriage. She and Austin might never move back into our home. They had a new home now. A new life, one in which I was barely involved.

As painful as it might have been to grasp, it was the truth and it was becoming more and more apparent that it wasn't going to change in the near future.

The time had come to let all the pain and bitterness go. I needed to focus on getting myself healthy, and one key component in that was learning to love unconditionally. Until I was able to do that, I knew I would never reach *the other side*, much less, lead my family there.

Chapter 19

A Ring and a Prayer

In January of 1990, Tammye and I moved to Oklahoma City where we became pastors of a small church. In the fall of that same year, we returned to Muskogee to attend to a business matter. We had a wonderful dinner with Tammye's mom and dad, then went to a revival service in my home church.

A good friend of ours happened to be in town preaching. In fact, over the years we had become very good friends. In many ways, he had been like an older brother to me. He always challenged me to think openly and remain willing to accept new paradigms. More than anything, his teaching on finance and faith inspired me in more ways than I could count.

During the most difficult seasons of our lives, he and his lovely wife remained supportive, even when others were not. They have exemplified the true meaning of friendship. To this day, we remain very close friends.

At the end of revival service that evening, my friend mentioned that he would not be receiving an offering that night; however, he felt led to mention that he believed several people were going to sow a special offering in the revival.

This wasn't that unusual in our church circles. It was, in fact, quite common to hear things of this nature. What did stand out was the voice on the inside of me. I heard the firm, but comforting voice of the Holy Spirit say to me, "You need to give an offering tonight. You need to give $300."

In all honesty, at that moment I was screaming,

"Get thee behind me, Satan!"

I'm an obedient man, but let's be real. I wasn't inclined to give up $300 without a fight. (The conversation was all happening on the inside of me, so no one else knew what was taking place.)

I replied, "Even if I wanted to give, I don't have $300."

Tammye and I were just getting started; thus, we were facing many of the same financial challenges that other new families face. Not to mention, our church was still very small and only able to provide a minimal salary for us. I seem to remember only having about $35 or so in my pocket on that particular night.

As I continued to argue my point of not having $300, the Holy Spirit gently reminded me that I did. (Any time you decide to argue with God, just know He's eventually going to win out.) *No, I don't have $300,*" I contended.

Then He said, *"What about the money you received at dinner this evening?"*

Hmmm . . . I guess I forgot about that. You see, I had sold a cook stove to a friend, and the money was given to me at dinner. Would you care to guess how much I sold it for? That's right, $300 cash.

Suddenly, the only dispute I could now wrangle was whether or not I would be obedient and give the offering or walk away with the cash in my pocket, knowing I was supposed to give it.

My response was simple and honest, *"Lord, I need that $300."* His response was direct, inspiring and challenging. *"You need what I'm going to do for you more than you need that money."*

With that in mind, I walked up and gave my $300 offering.

The events that happened over the next 30 to 45 minutes were absolutely mind-boggling. An atmosphere of giving engulfed the entire sanctuary. A spirit of faith enveloped the congregation and people began to give. Thousands of dollars were given without the prompting of any individual. It was truly an amazing moment. In all my years, I have only been part of a moment like this on a couple of occasions.

When it finally seemed to quiet down, my friend, the guest minister, asked me to come forward. As I did, he told the story of a time in his life when he was believing God for some larger than normal provision. During that time in his life, someone had given him a very large, beautiful diamond ring. From that time forward, he had worn the ring with a great appreciation for God's blessings and as a constant reminder of all that God wants to do for His children.

He then took the ring and placed it in my hand. He said because of my faith and obedience in giving in that offering, he was giving that very special ring to me. In such, I should always be reminded of the blessings and provision God has for me. And to never forget that He would always be with me.

It was such a significant moment. I bowed my head in gratitude as I pledged to never forget what had just happened. On top of receiving a new ring, as I was leaving the church that evening, someone gave me an envelope with $350 inside.

To recap, I had given the $300, then received a ring valued at several thousand dollars and received an envelope with $350 cash. I'd say that's a good trade.

Just as promised, God had done something so amazing, I would never forget that night.

From that time till now, I have often reflected back on that very important event. I have shared this story hundreds of times hoping to encourage others. When I wear the ring, people often comment about how beautiful it is, giving me another opportunity to tell them this powerful story.

Though I no longer wear the ring on a daily basis, I do wear it occasionally with a particular purpose in mind—to remind myself of the immense provision and blessing God has promised. Especially if I'm facing a challenging situation, I will wear it. It helps me to constantly reflect on God's promises. As a result, I consistently remind myself that I am not alone, for He is ever with me.

I have never forgotten His gentle words to me that special night, "You need what I'm going to do for you more than you need that money." I can tell you with great assurance, $300 could never buy the understanding and encouragement I received from giving that offering.

I'm sharing this story with you for several reasons, one of which is to acknowledge that we often find strength and encouragement from reflecting on certain moments or even particular objects that reflect distinct scenarios.

Much like a wedding ring, it neither defines nor solidifies a marriage. It does, however, serve as a symbol and constant reminder of the matrimonial covenant two people have entered into.

In the same regard, God set a rainbow in the sky as a symbol and constant reminder the earth would never again be destroyed by a flood.

Numerous times throughout history, we find where people constructed monuments, altars and other objects for this very reason—to bring remembrance.

Having been raised in a godly home with great parents, there were numerous spiritual elements that carried into my adult life.

My parents were very adamant that we attend church on a regular basis as well as that we remain involved in some area of service. In reality, it was usually many different areas of service.

We attended church every time the doors were open. In fact, there was a good chance we were the ones opening the doors and checking to make sure everything was ready for service. I can easily say I spent more time in church than any other place, with the obvious exceptions of home and school. Later on, I attended a private school that was located at our church; thus, I was right back at church.

When our home church was not having service, we usually found our way to a revival, a singing or some other type of service, hopefully within an hour or so of our home.

When we were younger, my brother and I were picked up by our uncle, then taken to the church to help him clean and make sure things were ready for Sunday. He would reward us with an ice cream cone and whatever change we found in between the seat cushions at the church.

I want you to grasp this picture. Our family spent a lot of time at the church. Not because dad was the pastor; he wasn't. Simply because we believed it was important to serve in any way we could.

I think we often underestimate the value of attending a good church and raising our children in that environment.

We certainly want the best for our children. We buy them the best sporting equipment and take them to all of the popular camps and tournaments, hoping they will excel. We invest in our children in every possible way as we should.

> ✌
> *I think we often underestimate the value of attending a good church and raising our children in that environment.*

Unfortunately, in our effort to help our children succeed in sports and other areas, we often find it easy to replace going to church in exchange for these extracurricular activities.

In no way am I implying that sports and other activities are bad. I am simply drawing an analogy to the obvious. Every family embraces a different set of values, and our priorities have changed as a society.

Sure, our family may have been a little different than others. Our family may have attended church more than most. Our family may have sacrificed many things in order to help the church. Then again, that's one thing I liked most about our family. God always came first.

I remember when I had to give up baseball in the fifth grade, because the coach decided to have practice on Wednesday evenings. That just wouldn't work for us. We had church. We certainly wouldn't be allowed to go play tournaments every Sunday either.

Please understand, I recognize life is a bit different now and not every congregation has a mid-week service. I also realize times have changed and our lives are more complex. Work schedules are different. Activities are more involved. Everything has changed over the years.

It is not my desire to offend you if you have chosen any of these activities over the church. With that in mind, I would caution you to maintain a healthy balance in your priorities and teach your children to do the same.

The importance of my family's church history is relative, because it will help you understand where I came from and how I was taught to call on God *every* time I had a crisis in my life. I was encouraged to remember and possibly set aside some token that would remind me, whenever I looked at it, that God was right there with me and that He would never let me down.

One such practice in our home was placing a picture on an open Bible as a reminder for us to pray for whoever was in that picture. We believed that God would answer our prayers and come to the aid of that person, and assist them with whatever problem they may encounter.

Much like looking at that ring, it was a constant reminder.

If you ever came into my parents' home and saw your picture on their Bible, you knew they had been praying for you.

I can't begin to tell you how many times my picture has been on their Bible. Oh, how thankful I am to know they have prayed over me on so many different occasions.

> *If you ever came into my parents' home and saw your picture on their Bible, you knew they had been praying for you.*

When I say they prayed, I mean they prayed. It wasn't some little ten-second prayer they read from a fortune cookie. They prayed until they felt like they had touched the throne of God. Even if it took all night, they didn't stop praying until they had a release. We called it praying through. You don't hear that term much anymore.

To this day, my parents continue to pray fervently, not only over my family, but for many others.

Any time I find myself facing a challenging decision or difficult season, I ask Mom and Dad to pray. On more than one occasion, I believe my life has been spared as a direct result of their prayers.

My mom will often let me know that she's been praying over me. She will never know how much I appreciate those prayers. She is a very small frame woman, with beauty and grace beyond words. Don't be fooled, however, by her physical stature. In the spirit realm, she is a giant.

On one occasion, I was traveling abroad. I was in a remote location with limited access to phone or Internet. When I returned home, Mom told me how she'd been praying over me day after day, night after night. At times, she stayed up all night praying. Only God may know the why, but I'm confident it held significant importance.

I love you, Betty Howell, and I thank God every day that He chose you to be my mom.

During our darkest season, after Tammye had moved out, a picture of our family remained on Mom and Dad's Bible constantly. They prayed over us every morning, every afternoon, every night and any other time they were reminded to.

They even organized several prayer gatherings where they brought others together to pray over us. I attended a few of those prayer meetings, but I have to admit, I was so discouraged I was barely able to pray.

On more than one occasion, people came to our house and prayed. It didn't matter if we were home or not, they still came and prayed for our family.

There were several times when one of my dearest friends came to the house in the middle of the night just to pray with me. I can't begin to tell you how thankful I am for friends like that. I can honestly say his encouragement and support helped save my life and my family.

On one particular occasion, Mom and Dad, along with a couple of friends, buried some prayer cloths around our property and anointed all the doors and windows in our home with anointing oil. (If this seems strange or odd to you, do a little research on the practice. It has biblical roots and very powerful symbolism.)

It's critical to note the importance of prayer. Whatever problem you may be facing, prayer will help you get through it. Prayer will help you overcome it. Prayer will help you find the strength and hope necessary for your journey.

As complicated as prayer may seem to some people, it is not. A friend once said, "How hard can it be to say, **'Help me'**?"

I want to encourage you right now, as you're reading these pages, ask God to help you. You don't have to say a bunch of *"thees"* and *"thous."* Just ask Him to help you. I can assure you, He will.

During that dark time, I found myself facing one of the loneliest and most challenging seasons of my life. Tammye and Austin were living in another house. The church was barely keeping the doors open. Finances were all but gone. Our life's savings had been depleted. Mom and Dad were both facing life-threatening diseases. Austin was struggling through his senior year and now my faith was under attack.

Never before had I questioned whether or not I trusted in God. This was an all-time low for me. If I died in my sleep or in a terrible car accident, I would have accepted it over this horrible pain.

Oddly enough, several things continued to stand out to me. Every time I saw our picture on Mom and Dad's Bible, I knew they were praying for us. Every time I saw that ring on my finger, I remembered the incredible night I received it and all that God did for us.

Over and over in my mind, the miracles and times of deliverance stood out. So many supernatural things had taken place right in front of our eyes.

How could God let us down in our greatest time of need?

It was difficult, frightful and discouraging. It was painful and humiliating. *The other side* seemed farther away than it ever had before.

So many times, I heard people say they gave up too soon and how they wished they would have tried harder and waited longer before walking away. I didn't want to add my name to that long list of regretters.

Regardless of how I felt and how hopeless things appeared, deep down in my heart, I knew God was still there. I knew He was still working on our behalf. I knew as long we held on to our faith, we could make it.

Our family was holding on to a ring and a prayer. Then again, considering this particular ring and prayer, we might just have a chance to make it.

(Even as I write these pages, there is a family's picture on my Bible; and I have worn the ring every day for quite some time. They are constant reminders that God is ever present and ever willing to come to our aid.)

Chapter 20

Three Little Words

It was the depressing summer of 2009, and we faced the most difficult challenge we had ever faced. Tammye and I had now been separated for nearly seven months. More accurately, we had been apart much longer than that.

Tattered and torn, we were functioning well below capacity. It seemed that a lifetime of winning and a legacy of stability had finally reached its breaking point. Everything that mattered seemed to drown in despair.

Thankfully, the tension had finally subsided. Anxiety had grown surprisingly low. Unfortunately, expectations were even lower. Even misery felt lonely in this darkness.

The stale summer breeze somehow weighed the balance of tomorrow's embrace. Would there be any contact? Would Tammye call or text? Were she and Austin okay? Did they need me? Should I drive by their house to see if they're home? They were still my family, or were they?

Friends and supporters that once held to every word we spoke, were nowhere to be found. Like sailors they jumped from our sinking ship. Then again, who could blame them? Our ship was sinking; and sinking fast, it was. Most were amazed we were still afloat. Somehow and for some reason known only to God, we were still alive.

Every day, we expected the next wave of disaster to sweep over the bough and finish off the nightmare we couldn't seem to rise from. Beat up, bruised and battered by the worst storm we had ever faced, we were ready to give up and let life, or death, claim our last fragment of hope.

As the grim reaper of devastation and destruction hovered over what was left of our weary souls, I felt compelled to do something drastic and completely uncharacteristic of someone in our plight.

I asked Tammye if she would be willing to go on a short trip with me.

I was both shocked and afraid when she said yes, even more so when she actually joined me for the ride to the airport.

We didn't know if it was a good idea or if it would turn out to be just another chapter in a wistful saga. Pushing my credit card to its limit, we bought two tickets and boarded a plane. We flew halfway across the country to an end we couldn't predict.

We landed in Ohio. We felt compelled to visit a couple who had persistently stood by us, regardless of how awful we acted out. Ironically, the husband was the same friend who had given me that very special ring some twenty years past. The same friend who had encouraged me to be open-minded. The same friend who had challenged me to believe anything was possible with God. Ultimately, the same friend who engaged us with the equivalent honesty as our counselors when he gently offered, "It may be time to walk away and start over."

It was the fourth of July, Independence Day in America. It was a parody of uncharted chasms. The endless depth of hopelessness that bled through our red, white and blue celebration was awkward at best.

A toast for freedom seemed highly insensitive for two who were bound with such despair.

We tried feverishly to hold our heads high. We were proud individuals, but we had nothing to be proud of in this season of lunacy. It was uncomfortable for everyone around us. Jokes were only funny as a courtesy to the moment.

We both recognized, this was most likely the last time we would ever take a trip together. Probably the last time we would ever share a flight, a hotel or a quasi-romantic dinner. Truthfully, the only thing remotely romantic about this trip was the setting sun in the background of our failing marriage.

I can't begin to imagine how our friends felt about us being there together. Somewhere deep inside, we felt as if God had strategically brought us to their home, within their grasp and under their covering.

Knowing that God had used them many times over the years to speak prophetically, not only into thousands of other lives, but also into ours. We hung on every word they said as if to say, "Go ahead, please tell us what to do. Help us find a way out of this dreadful dilemma."

Strangely, there was nothing even remotely prophetic coming from their lips. No great words of wisdom. No deep observations. No "Have you read this book?" or "Have you tried this ancient mantra?"

Then again, it may have been what they didn't say with their mouths, but openly displayed from their hearts. The way they embraced us with love and shared their faith in us still echoes in my memory.

They neither preached *to* us nor *at* us. They didn't tell us all the things we were doing wrong. They didn't even invite us to one of those special prayer gatherings that closely resembles an intervention.

They simply loved us—unconditionally. This gift would prove far more valuable than the ring ever could've attempted.

I learned a great lesson from these friends during this time. When you encounter someone who is at the end of their road, stop preaching at them. Just love them. It's the one thing they need most at that moment.

Why we were there still seemed to be a mystery. Nothing profound happened. Nothing worth etching in our memoirs. Nothing worth posting to our social media walls. Nothing, that is until . . .

In the midst of this silence, without any expectation; we heard the words that would forever correct our compass.

Profoundly clear and with laser-like precision, the words were deposited into the very core of our being. It felt as if a warm healing balm was being poured over us. Still distraught and weary, yet something or someone was trying to breathe hope back into us.

> *In the midst of this silence, without any expectation; we heard the words that would forever correct our compass.*

We couldn't begin to imagine how or how long it would take to embrace this rhema; but we believed these words were a lighthouse in the distance, guiding us to safety. It was perhaps the reason for this trip. We had flown far enough away from the darkness that we were finally able to glimpse a sliver of light penetrating the dense fog.

To this day, we are ever grateful for those gentle, yet overtly powerful words. The calming voice of comfort and peace, speaking life into our souls. It was as if an entirely new paradigm had exploded within us. Those three little words that became the prevailing wind in our sails. Without confusion or interference, we heard the words . . . *the other side*.

In an instant, we were reminded of the Bible story in Mark 4, where Jesus told the disciples to get in the ship, "We're going to the other side." It wasn't a request or a question. It was a proclamation.

As they made their journey across the open sea, a horrific storm arose and began to threaten their survival. The winds were howling at hurricane force. The waves were battering the vessel, each one crashing over the bow with greater determination than the last.

An obvious enemy had arisen with strategic purpose in denying their destiny. They would not be allowed to reach *the other side* without a miracle of extraordinary proportions. Several of the disciples were professional fishermen and thus, experienced sailors; yet they were no match for this tempest.

Frantically scouring the vessel, in the last moments before going under, they discovered Jesus doing something courageously unthinkable. He was sleeping in the bottom of the ship.

He was unconcerned that the vessel was taking on water and unafraid of the eminent danger. He had no fear that His legacy would end in brokenness and defeat, nor that the ship would descend to the depths. He simply slept like a baby in its mother's caress. Without a care in the world, He rested indisputably in the peace of His promise, "We're going to the other side."

Unimpeachably, we felt an immediate identification with this story of a raging storm and a floundering ship. We saw ourselves struggling, as it were, in the midst of a storm-tossed sea. We recognized the distinction being made between our dilemma and that of the disciples.

It was the next part of that Bible story that brought our first inkling of peace in more than a year.

Paralyzed with fear, the disciples woke Jesus and pleaded with Him to do something about the storm. Calmly and with great faith, He obliged.

As He made His way to the bow of their floundering vessel, He gazed deep into the heart of that storm. With violent winds and unceasing waves being hurled at Him, He commanded it to cease. He demanded, with great authority, the wind to be still and peace to reign over the waves.

Immediately, the wind lost its breath and the sea found its calm, allowing them to continue safely to *the other side*. Just as He had designed, they would fulfill a destiny of purpose and peace, setting free the demoniac from his chains of despair.

This was reminiscent of our story. We were those frightened sailors. The sinking ship was our marriage. The storm was an enemy assigned to destroy our home and thwart our destiny. It was exactly what that demonic spirit had spoken of the night he walked into our bedroom and proclaimed he would destroy our family.

> *Somehow, living inside our calamity were those three simple words . . . the other side.*

Somehow, living inside our calamity were those three simple words . . . *the other side*.

Hearing these words brought a somber moment. I'd like to tell you the heavens opened up and a bright light shown through the darkness. I'd like to tell you there was a burning bush or some other spectacular show of deity. I'd like to tell you we cried uncontrollably for hours, holding hands and declaring victory was at last ours.

It wasn't like that, however. It was deeper, more sovereign. It was definitive for sure. From the depths of darkness, those words rang through like a fog horn piercing the night. It was not a temperamental revelation. It was one of unparalleled distinction. One that transcended the shallows of our emotions and wove itself throughout the fabric of our existence.

Those words of life had been delivered straight from the throne of God, carried in the bosom of an angel of light. We were the target and our family the purpose.

We knew this was our last grasp at a future together. If we passed on this ember of possibility, we would sink faster than the Titanic. We had to embrace the prophetic word and lay claim to its potential. We had to find a way to lay aside our frustrations, our bitterness, our hurts and hang-ups. We had to reach one final time for the haven of harbor just beyond our horizon.

At last, we had something that had eluded us for as long as we could remember: HOPE.

We returned from the trip with a glimpse of peace. It was a small glimpse, but nonetheless a glimpse of something we hadn't seen in several years. We still struggled, and we still lived in separate homes. We still searched for answers, and we were still desperate. Although we didn't have much to hold on to, we had those three little words . . . *the other side.*

> *At last, we had something that had eluded us for as long as we could remember: HOPE.*

Would they indeed carry all that we needed to find safe passage? Would they live long enough in the depths of our despair, long enough to bring healing and restoration? Would we still feel the same hope once we were back home?

At this point, we couldn't even see *the other side*, much less know what it looked like. We had never been there. We had no distinct direction for getting there. How long would it take? Would there be more storms along the way? What would we do once we arrived? Where would we live? How would we live?

Those interrogations and a million more raced through our minds with every heartbeat.

We still had a myriad of delusions and dilemmas that had to be addressed. We were still living in two separate houses. We had trainloads of luggage dragging at our feet. We were out of money and deep in debt, still lost in a sea of despair.

All we had was the corrected compass brought by those three little words. It may not have seemed like much to those who peered through the windows of our soul, but to us it would have to be enough. After all, it was all we had.

> ❧
>
> *It may not have seemed like much to those who peered through the windows of our soul, but to us it would have to be enough. After all, it was all we had.*

It seemed like a dream. A place of peace. A land of tranquility. A haven of harbor for even the weariest vessels. A place where tattered and torn are maiden names.

The cry of our hearts lamented for the land we had never seen. Heaven help us to gain passage to this special place, our promised land. Give us the courage to speak to this storm, the faith to believe it will calm and the daring to rest in the bottom of our ship while morning breaks the darkness.

We longed for that secret place where dreams really do come true, *the other side*.

Chapter 21

Squeaky Brakes

It's not surprising that I chose a profession centered around solving problems. I enjoy finding creative solutions to everyday issues. From time to time a problem arises that is far beyond routine; nonetheless, every problem has an answer. Finding the right answer . . . now that's a whole new game.

For me, it started as a boy who liked to fix things.

Once upon a time, I bought a bicycle for a couple bucks at a garage sale down the street. Of course, my brother had been awarded a brand-new bicycle from our parents. That wasn't the case for me. I had to buy a salvage model. As if it wasn't bad enough growing up in hand-me-downs, I also had to ride a broken-down bicycle.

I remember after I brought that old bike home, I immediately started taking it apart. I took every piece and part off that old broken-down bike. I cleaned it, oiled it, greased it and fixed it. I even put a new coat of paint on that old thing. When I finished, it was the fastest ride in the whole neighborhood. The proud part for me was knowing that *I* fixed it.

Earning money was fairly simple in those days. I mowed grass, washed dishes or cashed in pop bottles for a nickel. (To this day, I still hate washing dishes.) A man up the street had a lawn mower for sale, $1. Yip, one whole dollar. I sauntered up the block and started my examination. "It just won't run," the man responded. Well, I gave him a dollar and headed home with my new project.

Just like everything else, I started taking it apart. Remember, I liked fixing things. When I got it all back together, it ran as good as new. Turns out, it only needed a good cleaning and a new spark plug. Isn't it interesting how many *"broken"* things in life can be fixed with a minimal amount of effort?

It was the beginning of my entrepreneurial adventure. *The other side* of my adolescent poverty was now within reach. I pulled that lawn mower behind my bicycle and mowed yards all over the neighborhood. All made possible with some imagination, determination and a few simple fixes.

Somewhere around fifteen or so, I moved on to a motorcycle. It wasn't a fixer-upper. It was brand new. I was so proud when Mom and Dad bought me that motorcycle. I rode that thing every day, rain or shine, cold or hot. It didn't matter. I could be found on that motorcycle.

After school, I'd fill up the tank with gas, about $1.50 and off I'd go. I drove down every road in the county. I'd ride until I ran out of gas, then I'd switch the tank over to the emergency reserve and head back home.

After a while, I noticed the brakes started squeaking. Man, was that annoying. It just kept getting worse and grew louder and louder. The obnoxious screeching went right through you. I don't have to tell you, it wasn't much of a winner when it came to being cool. The dogs would cry. My buddies would laugh and the girls, well, they were all gone by the time I came to a screeching halt.

Being the fixer that I am, I started looking for a fix. At that time, replacing the brakes was a little beyond my mechanical skills. I didn't have the money to take it to a professional, so I came up with another solution. At first I thought for sure I had invented a new way of fixing squeaky brakes.

I had watched my father spray a lubricant (WD-40) on things that squeaked, so I thought it would also work on my brakes. I grabbed Dad's can of spray and away I went. Common sense would tell you, if a little works good, then a lot should work great. So, I soaked those bad boys. Front and back. Top to bottom. Inside and out.

Now for the test. I fired up the yellow rocket and headed down the street. Man oh man, I could hardly believe how quiet those brakes were. No more screeching. No more squealing. I had done it. I had fixed those nasty brakes. Look out, girls! I'm back!

Everything was looking up. That is, until I came rolling back up to our house. The good news was, I was really quiet. Unfortunately, I had put so much lubricant on those brakes, they wouldn't stop. Not a lick. Nada . . . !

I plowed through the driveway, past the house, by the garage, around the swing set and smack dab in the middle of the bushes. I'm just glad they weren't rose bushes.

I thought I had solved a problem. All I had done was get rid of the squeak.

I thought I had solved a problem. All I had done was get rid of the squeak.

Too often, we do the same thing with our problems. Instead of taking the time and effort, or even spending the necessary funds to fix things the right way, we just get rid of the squeaking. The problem is still there; we've just masked its presence, momentarily.

The truth is, sooner or later we will have to deal with the problem. Ultimately, I had to have the brakes replaced on my motorcycle. Afterwards, they were both quiet and had good stopping power.

You can cover things up, but it doesn't solve the issues at hand. For most problems, we often have a decent idea of what's wrong and a general direction of how to fix it. Unfortunately, some problems are a little bigger than bicycles, lawn mowers and squeaky brakes.

If you have any hopes of reaching *the other side* of your dilemma, you will need to find the appropriate solutions. Some problems may be harder to solve than others, but they can be solved.

Nonetheless, every problem has a solution. Determination and patience will be a good start toward finding the answers you need.

Chapter 22

It's a Process

On July 5, 2008, I preached a message about "The Process." Little did I know my family was about to embark on the most challenging journey we had ever faced.

I do not believe God brought problems into my life to teach me a lesson and make me stronger. I do, however, believe that He gave me the strength and grace to successfully navigate through the very difficult days that lay ahead.

I find it ironic that exactly one year after preaching that message, we received the revelation that would ultimately transform our lives. That's when we heard those three little words.

Following that trip to visit our friends, we began the very difficult and lengthy process of rebuilding our family. Yes, I said *process*.

We live in a culture that wants everything instantaneously. A sort of microwave mentality.

Rather than stay home and cook a meal, we opt for the drive-thru at a fast food restaurant. Rather than grow our vegetables in the garden,

> *We live in a culture that wants everything instantaneously. A sort of microwave mentality.*

we let someone else do it for us; then we make our selection at the market.

We don't even change our own oil in the car. It's so much easier to pay someone else a few dollars to do it for us. After all, that keeps us from getting our hands dirty.

It's just easier to let someone else do the things that consume our time, especially the difficult stuff. Let them do the hard work while we enjoy the fruit of convenience.

If only we could do this when it comes to solving the most challenging dilemmas in our lives. Unfortunately, it doesn't work that way. It takes time to make a family. Time to raise a family. Time to weaken a family. Likewise, it takes time to rebuild it.

I believe this is one of the most common reasons families decide to walk away, instead of walking through the arduous process of rebuilding.

I've heard many families in crisis say, "It's just too hard to rebuild it. I don't think I can do it." While they may think divorce or walking away is an easier path, I can assure you, there's nothing easy about either course.

Tammye and I weren't looking for an easy road. We were looking for the right road. We weren't looking for the path of least resistance. We were searching for the best solutions to our dilemmas.

We knew it would not be easy. We knew it wasn't going to happen overnight. We knew it would be costly. We knew it would be the hardest thing we had ever attempted. We also knew it would be worth it in the end if we would stay the course.

Too many people think they can flip a switch and make everything good again. Too many think they can kiss and make up like they did in high school. It just doesn't work that way.

You didn't get into this dilemma overnight, and you're not getting out of it overnight.

More than likely, you can look back and see a pattern of things that weakened your relationship. You may notice things that happened over many months, or possibly over the course of several years, ultimately contributing to the crisis.

You need to make a determination right now, you're in it for the long haul. Find it in your heart to say it, "I won't quit. I will see it through till the end."

> ❧
> *You didn't get into this dilemma overnight, and you're not getting out of it overnight.*

Remember those sweet, mushy words you said at your wedding ceremony? "For better or for worse. In sickness and in health. For richer or for poorer. Till death do us part." That wasn't a suggestion. It was your commitment to stick together through the good times and the bad.

Tammye and I were well aware it would be a lengthy and difficult process to get to *the other side*.

You must understand, there is a process to life. A system, if you will. An order. A conforming, a transforming, an absolute that exudes its force on everyone and everything. Whether we like it or not, we are all subject to a process. You will learn, life is not only about the destination. It is equally about the journey.

When God made the heavens and the earth, He created a certain order. He put within the heavens and the earth a system, an order.

> *You will learn, life is not only about the destination. It is equally about the journey.*

We know that certain events will follow a particular order. The earth will take 24 hours to rotate one complete time on its axis. It will take 365.25 days to revolve around the sun one complete time. There are four seasons. Temperature and climate are particular to certain places.

There is an order, a system, a process. Even the process of creating the process was done in a particular order and process.

Ecclesiastes 3 notes these processes as seasons and clearly defines, *"...there is a season for everything."*

Numerous verses in the Bible mention the phrase, *"...in the process of time."* It is most certainly this "process of time" which challenges us. We want the end result to work in our favor; however, we seldom want to wait even one minute to achieve that result. We want it now. Expedite the process; remove me from the chaos, eliminate the struggle and give me the goods.

Noah engaged in the lengthy, time-consuming process of building the ark. Most agree, it took somewhere around 70 to 80 years to build the ark. It's entirely possible he could have taken some shortcuts and still found a way to survive. It's also important to remember, he was trying to save his entire family and a rather large collection of animals. It wasn't just about him.

Shortcuts often lead to disaster and failure. They rarely lead to long-term success. Had Noah opted for the shorter route, he may have found himself neck deep in the flood, rather than rising and riding above it.

Moses spent eighty years preparing to lead Israel out of slavery. At one point, he killed an Egyptian soldier who was beating a Hebrew slave. As a result, he was forced to flee to the country and go into hiding. He had the right motive, to help the slave; but he had the wrong timing, the wrong method and most definitely the wrong process.

Jacob agreed to work seven years for the right to marry Rachel. When her father gave him Leah instead, he agreed to work another seven years for Rachel. Think about that, he worked fourteen years for the right to marry the girl of his dreams. Genesis 29:20 NLT says, *"...his love for her was so strong that it seemed to him but a few days."*

She must have been a real princess, because I don't know anyone willing to wait fourteen years, much less work that long, just to marry a particular girl. In this day and age, people meet on a dating website, and they're ready to marry before the weekend is over.

Things of value, especially the growing and maturing processes of life, take time. Building a house takes time. Building a successful business takes time. Rebuilding your family also takes time.

Scientists have taught us that it can take several thousand years to make a natural diamond. It is a lengthy, time-consuming, pressure sensitive process whereby the earth produces one of the most valuable gems known to man.

It is also true that man has developed highly successful measures in which diamonds are created in the laboratory. Even still, this is a difficult, expensive and time-consuming process.

The length of time it takes to produce a fully grown, mature, fruit-bearing apple tree can often be several years. No one plants an apple tree in the yard, then wakes up the next morning expecting to pick fresh apples from it.

Even if your parents named you Jack, you must know there is no giant living in the clouds. No goose laying golden eggs. No golden harp playing your favorite songs and most definitely no magic beans that grow a beanstalk to the sky overnight.

Again, we need to remember that when we make things, there is an order, a process that we must follow. Whether making a cake, building a house, starting a business or developing a family. No matter how much we may want to get outside of the order, we are limited to following a particular process.

> *We may learn things along the way that make our life easier, but there are no shortcuts through the process of building (or rebuilding) a successful life.*

We may learn things along the way that make our life easier, but there are no shortcuts through the process of building (or rebuilding) a successful life.

The fortieth chapter of Isaiah references several stages in the process: walking, running and soaring, and of course, the all-important standing. We find ourselves in some aspect of this process continually. Today, you may be able to run, when tomorrow requires you to stand. Understanding the process and its intricacies is of great value.

Isaiah 40:29-31 tells us,

He giveth power to the faint; and to them that have no might he increaseth strength.

Even the youths shall faint and be weary, and the young men shall utterly fall:

But they that wait upon the LORD shall renew their strength; they shall mount up with wings as eagles; they shall run, and not be weary; and they shall walk, and not faint.[19]

Let's take a closer look at the "how-to" process as outlined in Isaiah. First, let's examine the all-important part, **to STAND**.

> "**Stand** *fast therefore in the liberty wherewith Christ hath made us free, and be not entangled again with the yoke of bondage*" *(Galatians 5:1 KJV).*

> "*Wherefore take unto you the whole armor of God,* **that ye may be able to withstand in the evil day, and having done all, to stand. Stand**. . . ."*(Ephesians 6:13-14 KJV).*

Sometimes, the best you can do is to STAND.

On many occasions, Tammye and I were so weak and so frustrated, we were unable to do much more than to **stand** by and wait on God to send strength and help. We didn't have an answer. We didn't know what to do. We weren't even in the best frame of mind to pray.

> *Sometimes, the best you can do is to STAND.*

I think people underestimate the value of patiently waiting, standing. Sometimes, we need to step back, take a deep breath and let life happen. In this case, we let healing and restoration happen.

Returning home from that trip to see our friends, we felt a sense of purpose and had a new sense of hope. Still, Tammye didn't move back home at that time. She continued to live in a different house. We continued to live separate lives. We were discussing our options and beginning to see some possibilities, but we were a long way from being ready to reconcile and even further from being whole again.

Secondly, Isaiah mentions a slightly faster pace, **to WALK**.

> "*...they shall* **walk,** *and not faint.*"[20]

> "*We* **walk by faith***, not by sight.*"[21]

*"**Walk in the Spirit**, and ye shall not fulfill the lust of the flesh."*[22]

*"If we live in the Spirit, let us also **walk in the Spirit**."*[23]

Progress is often a very slow, tedious measure. Walking may not win the race, but it can sure keep you from losing it.

Surely you remember the children's story about the tortoise and the hare. It's a valid lesson to keep in mind, especially when you think about rebuilding your family.

Even God exemplified this part of the process with Adam and Eve: *"And they heard the voice of the LORD God **walking** in the garden. . . ."*[24]

Enoch embraced this value, taking it to a special place. *"And Enoch **walked** with God...."*[25]

Noah, Abraham, Isaac, Joshua and Moses all understood the critical importance of **walking with God**.

The **WALK** may not appear to be the most glamorous and exciting part of your existence, but it is without question, one of the most important areas of your life. It is the most common part of the *process*. You may not run and soar every day, but you absolutely must **walk** it out every day.

> ❧
> *The walk of faith is a critical key to your breakthrough.*

The walk of faith is a critical key to your breakthrough.

The children of Israel WALKED out of Egyptian bondage. They WALKED through the Red Sea—on dry land. They WALKED across the desert. They WALKED across the Jordan River. They WALKED into the land of Canaan—the land of abundance. For them, this was *the other side*. They WALKED around the city of Jericho for seven days, before the walls came down.

Jesus and Peter WALKED on the water.

Jesus said to the man, sick of the palsy, *"...Arise, take up your bed and **WALK**."*

Luke 13:33 KJV delivers the words of Jesus: *"Nevertheless **I must WALK** to day, and to morrow, and the day following. . . ."*

I like the the way the NIV renders this verse: *"In any case, **I must press on** today and tomorrow and the next day."*

The literal translation of this says, to pursue the journey on which one has entered. Jesus' life was in danger, yet He held to the process while continuing on His journey.

If you intend to reach *the other side*, you must be fully committed to continuing on your journey, even if the pace becomes slow or stalled. You will hit snags and bumps in the road. You will have challenging days. You will have to press through and vow to continue.

Tammye and Austin Come Home

It was Labor Day weekend when Tammye and Austin moved back into our family home. As much as it was a day of apparent victory, it was equally a move that brought great concern. It was a risky decision to bring our family back under one roof at this time. Our counselors advised us to hold off a few more months. If it didn't work, it could prove to be one of the worst decisions we had ever made.

We were a long, long, long way from *the other side*, but at least we were making progress. We had no idea what *the other side* would ultimately look like, but we were convinced it would be worlds better than the hell we had been living in.

Even though our counselors had given up their optimism that we could make our marriage work, we still continued our weekly sessions. We learned to talk things out and listen to whatever advice they had for us.

We continued reading a handful of very helpful books, learning more and more about ourselves every day. It was a process whereby we learned things about ourselves we really didn't want to know, much less acknowledge.

We discovered things about our family history that pointed to areas where we struggled. We uncovered hidden skeletons, many of which we had subconsciously buried in hopes they would never be exhumed.

We managed to restructure numerous areas of our lives. We changed the way we connected with friends and co-workers. We changed phone numbers and emails. We changed the way we conducted ourselves in ministry. We changed many of our habits. We even found it helpful to change a few of our friends.

We also changed the way we argued. Yes, that's what I said—the way we argued. We learned it was okay to disagree with each other and completely permissible to voice our disapproval. With that in mind, we learned a better, nonaggressive, nonthreatening way to do this.

We found it very helpful to be able to discuss the most delicate matters, especially when we learned constructive ways to communicate. To this day, we still offer up several of the once delicate phrases that allowed us to voice our opinions during the rebuilding season. Phrases like, *"What I heard you say was . . ."* and *"This is how that makes me feel . . ."* or *"What I would like you to know is . . . ."*

Again, it wasn't easy and it didn't happen overnight. It was a process, and a long one at that.

Next in Isaiah's process, is **to RUN**.

*"They shall **run**, and not be weary. . . ."*[26]

*"Let us lay aside every weight, and the sin which doth so easily beset us, and **let us run with patience** the race that is set before us."*[27]

It's important to note, if you're going to run, and expect to win, you will need to lay aside some of the things you've been holding on to. I've learned, every sin is obviously a weight, even though every weight is not a sin. Regardless, if it's holding you back, lay it down.

Notice, even when the process speeds up, it still requires patience.

"...Let us run with patience. . . ."

This is often where the rebuilding effort gets derailed. Things have gotten a bit easier. There aren't as many arguments. The really bad days seem to have gotten fewer and farther in between. There is a sense of normalcy that has returned to our routine. Yet quite often, this is where a false sense of security often finds a home in our thoughts.

> *Notice, even when the process speeds up, it still requires patience.*

At this point, we're no longer walking on eggshells and no longer guarding our feelings or weighing out our words before letting them fly. If we're not careful, we will allow some of the same bad habits that got us into trouble to come right back. I can guarantee, trouble isn't far away, and it's waiting for any opportunity to make its presence known again.

Philippians 2:16 offers, *"Holding forth the word of life; that I may rejoice in the day of Christ, that I have not **run** in vain, neither laboured in vain."*[28]

The Amplified Translation of this verse states, *"I did not **run** [my race] in vain nor labor without results."*[29]

How sad it is when people are well on the road to recovery, then allow foolish and careless mistakes to destroy all the hard work that's gone into rebuilding the relationship. You must be patient! Even though things are getting better, don't get in a hurry. Healing has a natural pace.

> ❧
>
> *Even though things are getting better, don't get in a hurry. Healing has a natural pace.*

Our lead counselor thought Tammye was moving home way too soon. In hindsight, I would probably agree. We could've benefitted from a few more months of living apart, taking the opportunity to continue working on "us" as "individuals" without the stress of managing our relationship under the same roof.

If I could give you one solid bit of advice about rebuilding your family, I'd say, "Don't get in a hurry. Let time offer its value to the healing process."

If you truly want your family to last a lifetime, recognize it takes a lifetime to build a life.

"Through patience, a ruler can be persuaded. . . ."[30]

Last, Isaiah spoke of **SOARING like an eagle**.

He said, *"They shall mount up with wings as eagles. . . ."*[31]

To SOAR like eagles is a sign of strength and purpose. It's a mark of superiority. This part of the process most certainly doesn't happen overnight. In the same regard, this part of the process is the least experienced by the vast majority. Partly because it also has a direct correlation to our maturity. You see, baby eagles don't fly. They sit in the nest and let Mom and Dad take care of their every need. Unfortunately, this is where most people want to live, thus they never grow to full maturity.

Though it is completely possible, and well within reach, most do not ascend to this level. For various reasons, too many get hung up with other things and never fully reach the potential of *the other side*.

Popular opinion, social sentiment, old-fashioned guilt, pride and immaturity are often the biggest contributors to limiting our newfound success. The world wants to convince you that you can never be what God called you to be, and you can never reach your full potential. The enemy wants to tell you, "Even if you do somehow manage to reach *the other side*, you won't be worth much. You'll always be marked. You'll always carry a scar. You'll always be viewed as damaged goods."

I'm here to tell you, nothing could be further from the truth. You can be more successful than ever. You can reach more dreams than you ever imagined. You can go further! You can fly higher! You are beautiful, strong and wise! You are an eagle!

You've gained an understanding about life that gives you special insight. You may have been knocked down, but you got back up and found the courage to rebuild your life.

Eagles learn to ride the winds of adversity and use them to their advantage. Eagles use the force of a storm to fly high. They love to fly on windy days. They have even been seen by airline pilots flying thousands of feet up in the sky.

That's the new you. You are an eagle. Your life can be better than before. Your marriage can be stronger than before. You've learned to

> *You've gained an understanding about life that gives you special insight. You may have been knocked down, but you got back up and found the courage to rebuild your life.*

overcome the greatest adversity. You're not the same person you once were. You're different, stronger and better.

What the enemy tried to use as a setback, God used as a setup. Declare it right now, ***"My best days are ahead of me!"***

You can get to *the other side*, but understand, getting there is a process.

> *Dear brothers and sisters, when troubles come your way, consider it an opportunity for great joy. For you know that when your faith is tested, your endurance has a chance to grow. So let it grow, for when your endurance is fully developed, you will be perfect (mature) and complete, needing nothing.[32]*

Tammye and I were at a place in the process where we could finally see the progress.

We had been challenged. We had been attacked. We had been beat up, lied to, lied about, pushed around, knocked down, run over and left for dead. Thankfully, we were far from dead. We may not have been completely well, but at least we felt alive again.

We continued to embrace the process, in all its stages, for several more years. Even now, we still caution ourselves not to get entangled with areas that once caused us problems. We live differently. We move differently. We think differently. We talk differently. After all, we are different.

In whatever state you find yourself today, understand there is a process to get you through today and tomorrow and the next day. Everything you do will involve the process. If you're starting a family, it is a process. If you're rebuilding a family, it's a process. If you're building a ministry, it's a process. If you're building a business, it's a process. Whatever you're doing, it's a process.

What you're doing may change and how you're doing it may change; but there will always be a process involved.

Determine to embrace a process that will bring positive results.

For our light and momentary troubles are achieving for us an eternal glory that far outweighs them all. So we fix our eyes not on what is seen, but on what is unseen, since what is seen is temporary, but what is unseen is eternal.[33]

> ❧
>
> *What you're doing may change and how you're doing it may change; but there will always be a process involved.*

Focus on the things that matter. Pay attention to what's important.

All great leaders embraced the process and allowed it to shape their destiny. Noah, Abraham, Jacob, Joseph, Moses, Joshua, Peter, Paul and many more great leaders.

It's much like harnessing the power of a river. Harnessed correctly, it produces electricity, provides controlled irrigation and allows for safe navigation of the waterways.

If you refuse to allow the situation to destroy you, the process will prepare you. If your faith doesn't fail, the process will reward you. If your perseverance and patience endure, the process will mold you. If you understand the process, you'll embrace the promise and reap its reward.

"Finishing is better than starting . . . ."[34]

As survivors of a tumultuous journey to *the other side*, we are humbly thankful for the wisdom and life lessons learned throughout the process. Today, we are wiser, stronger and better equipped for the challenges of life.

Still, there are times when standing is more needed than soaring. It is the process which has helped us to understand the difference.

Regardless of where you may be today in the process, He is ever willing to assist you and give you the strength, grace and mercy that you need to make it through.

I give you all the credit, God—you rescued me and got me out of that mess, I yelled for help and you put me back together, and made me healthy. God, you pulled me out of the grave and gave me another chance at life.[35]

God used a process to do all of this.

> ❧
>
> *If you refuse to allow the situation to destroy you, the process will prepare you. If your faith doesn't fail, the process will reward you. If your perseverance and patience endure, the process will mold you. If you understand the process, you'll embrace the promise and reap its reward.*

Chapter 23

Enemies Unseen

Have you ever been in a place all alone; yet you felt like someone was also there with you? Someone watching you? Someone paying attention to everything you did and said? Even though you couldn't see them with the naked eye, you were convinced they were there?

You may be inclined to say yes. In fact, you may even be inclined to accept that God or an angel were there with you. To that end, I could agree.

Jesus said He would never leave us nor forsake us. The Psalmist David rendered in the 23rd, *"...goodness and mercy shall follow me all the days of my life."* [36] Some have contended that *"goodness"* and *"mercy"* could be angels. Psalm 46:1 offers, *"God is a very PRESENT help in trouble."* [37]

If you believe God or His angels can be present, regardless of whether or not you can see them (and I certainly hope you believe this), then I ask you to consider the possibility of a different presence—the presence of Satan and his cohorts. I believe this too is possible.

We struggle to acknowledge the presence of an evil force, yet we are quick to blame God when something goes wrong. Insurance companies offer up the blame for natural disasters as an *"act of God."* The damage may be the result of a supernatural influence, but I can assure you God is not the cause.

The desire to find blame and assess fault is inherent in our culture. Children are quick to blame their siblings. Parents are ready to blame their children, and everyone is ready to blame someone else.

Why is it that we struggle so much to acknowledge the presence and influence of an evil force?

If you believe the Genesis account of creation, regardless of your position that it is either factual or allegorical, the story reveals the presence of both God and Satan. Eve is depicted as being coerced by the serpent, a representation of Satan, into partaking of the forbidden fruit. As a result, both she and Adam were then banished from the garden—a consequence of their ill-fated decision.

> *Why is it that we struggle so much to acknowledge the presence and influence of an evil force?*

We have little trouble recognizing the presence of Satan in this story, yet when we talk about other biblical accounts we struggle to acknowledge his influence. Consider in the story of Sampson and Delilah; regarding Sampson's failure, we place the blame squarely on him and Delilah. When we consider Judas and Peter, both who betrayed Jesus, they are both considered weak and flawed, as are the assumptions of blame in many other relevant stories.

When Jesus was alone in the wilderness for forty days, was it not Satan himself who came and tempted Jesus? We don't blame God for this temptation. Why then are we so fast to blame Him for all the other times someone is tempted? James reminds us, *"... When you are being tempted, do not say, 'God is tempting me.' God is never tempted to do wrong, and he never tempts anyone else."[38]*

It is highly probable, you too have been blamed for any number of problems and failures, thus giving you the unenviable label that associates you to the failure.

I will agree, we must be accountable for our actions, our words and even our thoughts. I would also contend there are unseen influences that encourage us to those positions and the subsequent actions.

I've often said, no normal person wakes up on a bright sunny day and declares, *"Today is my day to go out and become a failure."* It's just not how we are wired.

We are programmed to succeed, to win and to ultimately overcome. A glass of water is healthy in its purest form; yet, introduce toxins or parasitic organisms into that glass of water and its value immediately diminishes. Much in the same way, negative influence corrupts and corrodes even the purest of hearts.

> *We are programmed to succeed, to win and to ultimately overcome.*

You can't walk into the nursery at a hospital and pick out the losers, thugs, liars and cheaters from among the newborns. They're all beautiful little bundles of life. They're adorned with peace and purity of heart, radiating destiny and divine purpose.

However, as they grow through the different stages of their development, outside forces influence them into thinking, talking and acting a particular way.

Many will grow up to be just like their parents. Partly because their parents have more opportunity to influence them than any other person. As they grow older, they may or may not decide to be like their parents for various reasons. Thus, they may adopt the characteristics of other influences.

What often goes unnoticed is the unseen influence of spiritual forces.

We've all seen the cartoons depicting a person trying to make a decision. An angel sits on one shoulder and the devil on the other, both trying to convince the person of a particular view: one good, one evil.

> *What often goes unnoticed is the unseen influence of spiritual forces.*

Believe it or not, this isn't too far from the truth. Somewhere, somehow, an unseen force has offered its influence to you for the purpose of this moment in your life.

This is one of the many reasons we should use great discretion in regards to the information we allow into our life through our sensory gates. The information will ultimately be used to influence us in one direction or another.

Various forms of media, culture, social environment, relationships, music, movies and so much more offer both subtle and obvious influences. Some of these influences can lay dormant for years before being called upon to move you in a particular direction.

Many of these influences are sown deep into the fabric of our families creating lifestyles, belief systems and genealogies that perpetrate the continuation of a particular influence.

The Apostle Paul spent a great deal of time in his writings to the early believers admonishing them of the presence of unseen influences.

He often linked these influences to spiritual powers, both good and evil.

He remarked of Timothy's faith, *transcending from his mother and grandmother.*[39] He was acknowledging that both had made deposits into Timothy's character. Thus, his mother and grandmother must have made a conscious effort to account to him spiritual matters.

I challenge you to impart to your children things that encourage and uplift them. Give them an environment conducive to strengthening their faith rather than destroying it.

Paul also notes the presence and influence of demonic powers and the bondage they attempt to introduce. These influences begin in our thoughts and if left unchecked, they produce imaginations or meditations. If they're allowed a home in our imaginations, they will produce strongholds or bondages in our life. We might say it differently than Paul. We might be inclined to call them bad habits or possibly addictions.

You may be thinking drug addiction or alcoholism have no relevant relationship to demonic influences. I submit they do. Notice the signage on the liquor store, *"Wine and **spirits**."* Many drugs cause a sense of euphoria and hallucination, closely associated with the mind's ability to create extreme *imaginations*.

Without question, there are numerous chemical and physiological associations to consider. Likewise, there are a plethora of spiritual forces offering their influence in these matters. The ultimate goal of the enemy is to destroy us. Jesus said, *"The thief comes only to steal and kill and destroy. . . ."*[40]

Thankfully, Jesus went on to say, *"I have come to give you life, really abundant life."* The word for "life" is the Greek word *zoe*, which simply means the God-kind of life. By a matter of simple faith in Christ, you are a candidate for the God-kind of life, free of any and all bondage and addiction.

This passage is further evidence of two distinct influences in our lives: God, the giver of life; and Satan, the thief, killer and destroyer.

Consider the mistakes and failures in your life. How did you arrive at the position or condition to make the decisions involved in that matter? I submit you were influenced by someone or something, whether seen or unseen. The hidden agenda to seduce you into making detrimental decisions should be obvious and apparent. Unfortunately, it can be difficult to discern this influence, as it is often cloaked in palatable pleasures.

I am a believer in many of the methods used to assist people in overcoming various problems. I am further convinced that most, if not all of these problems, have a spiritual influence at the core.

The ability to recognize, identify and understand the nature of a problem is paramount to resolving the issue.

Thankfully, there are some brilliant doctors, pastors and counselors who are able to identify many of the underlying conditions that cause a person to struggle. It is then possible to offer supportive and substantive measures conducive to living a balanced life.

> *The undeniable presence of evil influence in our world must not be overlooked.*

The undeniable presence of evil influence in our world must not be overlooked.

It is this evil influence of greed that causes an educated businessman to leave his routine of successful business principles and succumb to the delusional lure of gambling. It is the misaligned attraction of lust that draws a godly mother away from the inclinations of a peaceful home into the dark void of adultery.

It is the presumptuous grasp for power and popularity that coerces a balanced leader into the deceptive horrors of hubris and narcissism. The doctor into drug addiction. The pastor into pornography. The father into alcoholism. The daughter into prostitution.

These are not ordinary, balanced, well thought out, lucid decisions of discipline. Rather, they are the result of unhealthy, unnatural, ungodly and often unseen influences moving individuals to act in ways they would otherwise not be inclined to act.

We still may have to pay a price for our indiscretions, but we should at least be willing to recognize the demonic power that systematically manipulated us into those disappointing choices.

Learning to recognize this will do much more than simply share the blame. It gives us the understanding that good people sometimes do bad things.

It's important to note, bad decisions do not readily indicate a bad person. Failure is never final, and most importantly of all, God's love for that person is still the same—unconditional.

Once we are able to recognize the tricks and tactics the enemy is employing against us, it is easier to defend against that influence.

Paul mentions standing against the "wiles" of the devil.[41] The word translated "wiles" literally means "cunning arts, deceit, craft and trickery." One translation renders it the "strategies of the devil," while another relates, "the devil's schemes."

> *Failure is never final, and most importantly of all, God's love for that person is still the same— unconditional.*

The Apostle Paul reminds us *"not to be **ignorant** of Satan's devices, lest he gain advantage of us."*[42] Still others translate it this way: *"Not to let him outsmart or outwit us, for we are familiar with his schemes."* The word "ignorant" in this verse literally means "to be without understanding."

If I told you I was going to slap you, you would take evasive measures to avoid being slapped. Likewise, once you have an understanding for the strategy that is being used to influence you, you are able to take preventative measures against it.

I realize this sounds considerably easier than it actually may be. Nonetheless, a lucid understanding of the enemy's strategy against you will yield an essential tool in overcoming, thwarting and destabilizing the devious plot.

James 4:7 KJV admonishes, *"Submit yourselves therefore to God. Resist the devil, and he will flee from you."*

Don't overlook nor underestimate the authority you have as God's child to resist the vehement attacks of the devil. You can defeat these attacks and be victorious on every occasion.

To this day, Tammye and I still encounter challenges and struggles that attempt to introduce an unsettling and tormenting spirit into our home. Recognizing the origin, strategy and purpose of this influence; we are more prepared to defend against the assault.

I'm often reminded of the night that demonic presence came into our bedroom and declared he would destroy our family. The fury of hell was unleashed in an effort to cause as much destruction and pain as possible.

As I have described, in the months and years to follow, unseen forces assaulted our family with a barrage of malicious, venomous, malevolent strategies all designed with one purpose in mind, our demise.

It's important to note these demonic strategies will even target friends and family members close to you in order to accomplish the ultimate goal—a total annihilation of your God-given destiny and the eternal damnation of your soul. This is often accomplished through a myriad of various strategies. Enough so, that it is often difficult to tell exactly which direction the attack is coming from. This brings confusion, heightens frustration and fosters an overall sense of helplessness.

Beyond the dilemmas of our marriage, finances, ministry and careers, there were also vicious attacks on other members of our family during this same time frame.

While driving home from Bible college, Austin was overrun by a semitruck. He had stopped at a traffic light on the highway entering our city. The driver of a semitruck was traveling too fast and was unable to stop, thus he plowed through Austin's vehicle, a small Honda Civic. The collision pushed Austin's car through the intersection and into oncoming traffic. His car was completely destroyed.

Only by God's grace and the protection of His angels was Austin's life spared. Amazingly, he walked away.

On the outside, this may have looked like nothing more than a terrible traffic accident. At its core, it was a sinister attack by unseen demonic forces attempting to take Austin's life and thwart his destiny.

On several different occasions over a relatively short time, my mother became dreadfully ill. Time and again, the doctors were unable to diagnose the cause, thus making it inherently difficult to offer a cure or plan of healing.

On one particular occasion, Mom was in the hospital battling for her life. She recalls a man walking into her room in the middle of the night, dressed in professional attire. He said, "I'm here to let you know everything will be okay. Don't worry, you will be fine." Never before and never since did she ever see this man again. It remains her belief that he was an angel sent by God to reassure her the enemy would not be allowed to steal her life.

In that same hospital stay, Mom was serenaded with Christmas carols. She could hear them coming from the hallway outside her room. When she enquired about the singing, the nurses informed her no one had been there singing.

Believe what you will. Mom believes the angels were singing for her that night to bring comfort and peace.

Shortly thereafter, Mom walked out of that hospital room, healed and whole.

Not long after this, my father found himself in a battle for his life when he suffered a massive heart attack. Unstable and unable to be transported to the specialist an hour away, he was forced to undergo immediate surgery in our small local hospital. Once again, an unseen enemy had targeted our family.

A few months later, Dad survived a second heart attack. Tests revealed 99 percent of a major artery was blocked. Multiple doctors remarked how unusual it is for a person to survive this situation.

Thankfully, Dad survived both attacks. Today, he and my mom are both healthy and whole. They are living testimonies of God's grace and mercy. In one of Dad's follow-up appointments, the doctor noted, "From a medical standpoint, it's difficult to tell there's even been one event, much less two. There is almost no traceable damage."

These were distinct attacks on other members of our family, all within a short period of time, all with the identical purpose of destroying our family. All from the same devious, calculating, evil enemy. All intended to rob our family of the destiny and legacy God had promised.

I share these stories, not to glorify or magnify the enemy, but rather to expose him for who he is—a liar, thief, manipulator, murderer, monster, villain, adversary and accuser. More so, it's imperative to remember he is a defeated foe.

The Word declares Satan and all his cohorts have been defeated and dethroned. It further declares they are under our feet as children of God. We need to continually declare and decree God's Word over our lives; as well as the lives of our family. It is important we make proclamations of truth, such as, "If God is for me, who dare stand against me?" and "Greater is the power living on the inside of me, the power of God."

During those hard times, Tammye and I routinely declared and decreed that we would rise from our despair. We proclaimed we would ascend from our delusion, navigate the seas of adversity and arrive safely on *the other side*.

Though our journey was not yet complete, we were boldly and confidently moving in the direction of our destiny. We purposed to enjoy every sunrise and sunset as we set our sails in the wind. We were confident, if we remained persistent and refused to quit, we would get to *the other side*.

Although it was a long and difficult process, Tammye and I found ourselves in a unique orientation. We were finally able to catch a glimpse of dry land, and it held a strong resemblance to the paradise of which we'd been dreaming. It was a place of peace and tranquility. A place of healing and health. A place where we were no longer victims, but victors.

With each new sunrise, we grew closer still. The gale of desperation had turned to a fresh breeze of resolve. Slowly, but surely, the storm had given way to placidity. The distant horizon seemed to glow like an ancient city of gold. This was no mirage. It was no illusion. It was our new home, and we could see it more clearly than ever before.

Chapter 24

The Journey

Tammye was home, but we were not whole. Optimistic, but not euphoric. We were committed to the effort, but often struggled to find strength for the journey. We were well aware of the arduous labor yet needed to arrive safely in harbor.

Every day was not peaceful. Night held no promise of tranquility, and every conversation held the distinct possibly of erupting in vile and contempt. It was as if we were walking on ice; very, very thin ice.

Surviving to this point had been a very difficult challenge. Continuing on would be anything but easy.

We could not allow ourselves to become distracted with any measure of progress we felt we had attained. We still had work to do, and plenty of it.

Too often we become fixated on an end, the destination, without giving heed to the greater purview of intended providence.

It is the journey that should inspire us, more so than the destination that consumes us. Our

> *It is the journey that should inspire us, more so than the destination that consumes us.*

path to freedom is just that, a path. Our voyage to *the other side* is equal in its parallel.

There will always be a journey, a voyage, a quest. Likewise, *the other side* will always reside at the edge of our scope. This journey called life is much more than we often consider.

It's been noted, the hash on our gravestone represents more than the dates on either side. Our existence is far beyond our birth and subsequent death. It is the colorful life in between that yields our legacy.

We think of the moment we were born into this world as the *"beginning"* of our journey; yet for our parents, this moment was the fulfilling of a significant part of their life—far from the beginning.

At times, it is difficult to tell where we are in our personal journey. The beginning, the middle or the end. What seems like the beginning to some resembles the middle for others.

Our journey begins with small moments that are captivating and worthy of documenting: our first steps, our first words, our first bicycle ride and subsequently, our first bicycle wreck. The journey later yields our first car, our first speeding ticket, our first accident, and so on and so on. Through life the journey continues.

> *Our existence is far beyond our birth and subsequent death. It is the colorful life in between that yields our legacy.*

Eventually, no one is watching us take those steps. More importantly, no one cares that we can ride a bike or drive a car. Instead our journey has become ordinary and common, or so it seems.

Yet at some point, our journey takes an unsurprising and significant turn. We find ourselves uniting our journey with that of someone so special that life itself seems to begin all anew.

The excitement of laughing, loving and learning all about another person has a way of mesmerizing us. We become engulfed in all that they are, as if we're overcome with a tribal herb, giving way to hallucinations and fantasy.

For reasons unknown, we adopt new ideologies, new buzzwords, new mannerisms and idiosyncrasies. We also develop new habits—both good and bad. Our journey somehow becomes so interconnected, we lose focus of where we are, who we are and whose journey we're on. Magically, this new journey of two imperfect people becomes "ours" and suddenly life rings of perfection.

Before long, another new journey begins. This time it's the innocent faces of our miniatures, crying out for guidance from parents who are barely old enough to vote, much less capable of influencing the path of little feet. Nonetheless, we manage the courage to strike out on the voyage.

Life is fun and exciting. Trips here and there, taking in the sights and sounds of a vast universe. Small journeys which add up to the complexity of something much greater.

Church programs, school plays, ball games, amusement parks and the like now make up a journey of what has become the futility of routine. There are so many stories, so many adventures and so many life-filled days.

Certainly, there are parts of our journey we'd like to forget. Days of sadness, frustrations and regrets. Friendships that fell apart. Family members lost in their own journey. Challenges, hard times, growing up and growing old.

At last, our body will grow weary until finally, the journey begins to slow.

It is then we stop the merry-go-round for a moment to realize how many years have come and gone—40, 50, 60 years and beyond. How could it have gone by so fast? Where did it all go?

This is the place the journey becomes vastly different. The children, grandchildren and greats all come to visit. They've found their own journey now, and we're only a small part of all that is going on in their world.

We find comfort as we watch them learn and grow. We quietly observe as they navigate the twists and turns of their own story. We cry and pray for peace as they encounter storms beyond their understanding. We cautiously offer solace and counsel as we wait patiently for the right moment to say, "I know exactly how you feel. I was once in the same place as you."

As time marches forward, trips to the store are now to pick up a new prescription. Trips to the mall have become trips to the doctor. A good holiday is one not spent in the hospital with a lingering illness. Yes, life has definitely changed. This part of the journey here on earth is almost over, and we're okay with that. We're so tired. We just want to rest.

If we're remotely normal, this will be our story.

For Tammye and I, our journey together began when we were barely out of high school. Sadly, we realized that our journey had taken a few wrong turns and now required substantial course correction if we ever hoped to share the joys of growing old together.

We acknowledged that correcting our course would not be easy. We fully understood the immense scope of what our reconciliation would necessitate. We embraced the undeniable truth that our journey would never carry us to *the other side* unless we were willing to engage in a process capable of delivering us to our intended goal.

Our legacy would not be complete if left in defeat. We had too much potential to allow an evil enemy to destroy our destiny. We refused to allow it to be stained and thwarted by arrogance, ignorance and immaturity. We were determined to finish our journey in peace, regardless of the cost.

If we look back to the story of Jesus and the disciples, once they reached *the other side*, a man possessed with thousands of devils came running from his home in the tombs. Suddenly, it all became clear to the disciples.

The voyage had not been for their purpose alone, but for this man. The journey carried a far greater objective than simply sailing across an open sea. Had they failed in their quest, had they succumbed to the fierceness of the storm, this man would not have been delivered from his tempest. His family would have never been restored. His journey would have never reached its greatest potential.

Rising from deep within Tammye and I was the recognition that our journey too held greater purpose than we could ever have imagined. On *the other side* of our storm, others would certainly be waiting for a fresh resolve and a glimpse at their own sense of peace. Our journey held a renewed purpose, and we needed to embrace it.

Never get so distracted by the destination, you fail to embrace the purpose in going.

There will always be another journey, a new voyage filled with conviction and design, as well as a new storm of historic proportions that will try to hold you back from fulfilling dreams and sharing hope.

> ✦
>
> *Never get so distracted by the destination, you fail to embrace the purpose in going.*

Once Jesus had delivered the demoniac from bondage, He said something monumental to the disciples: "We're going back to *the other side*." This time *the other side* was a previous destination. Once again, it represented the fulfillment of a destiny far and beyond what was immediately visible to the naked eye.

Tammye and I prayed for the day we would be healed and healthy again. A day where we would find the strength and courage to help rescue others lost at sea, facing a peril beyond their scope. Our journey together has been anything but normal. Unfortunately, the dysfunction experienced in our home is far too common among other families.

Tammye and I believed *the other side* would someday serve as a peaceful reminder of where we came from and all that we went through. A journey littered with twists and turns, ups and downs and God's immeasurable grace. Hopefully, sooner rather than later, we would stand boldly on the shores of a land secure and strong, knowing that nothing and no one could stop us.

We often reflect on the words of Jesus. "With men this is impossible; but with God all things are possible."[43]

Chapter 25

Swimming Upstream

The steps we take each day are critical to our overall path in life. If we take one or two bad steps, it may not be devastating as long as we are are quick to correct our path. If we make one or two bad decisions, it may not completely thwart our development, especially when we refuse to allow it to become more than that, just one or two.

In any scenario, God is there to help us stay on track or restore us back to the right path, should we stray.

The Psalmist David said:

The Lord directs the steps of the godly. He delights in every detail of their lives. Though they stumble, they will never fall, for the Lord holds them by the hand.[44]

When we take an errant path, or take a series of bad steps, it can most definitely lead to destruction and devastation. It is crucial that we make good decisions and be diligent in maintaining balance with our priorities. It is

> *In any scenario, God is there to help us stay on track or restore us back to the right path, should we stray.*

often a misalignment in priorities that initially leads down a path of destruction.

The immense influences and routine bombardment of ideas, theories and opinions are a constant threat to our path. Friends, family, media, social networks, traditions and cultural impressions are immanently shaping our lives and thus have an enormous effect on the way we live—right or wrong.

It is imperative to evaluate not only our steps, but also the ideology behind our steps; the belief system that tells us what to do, how to do it, when and where. Thankfully, we have an inner compass that alerts us when we stray off course, otherwise known as our conscience—that still small voice of our spirit man, seeking to lead us in the right direction.

More and more, it seems the values of our society are eroding away. It seems popular opinion is winning out over truth and moral high ground. Prevailing trends are dictating a path of little or no resistance. This, in turn, creates a situation where our social support system is skewed, leaving a vacuum in our culture that systematically seduces us into questionable activities, conversations and lifestyles we may otherwise not embrace.

It's not hard to see that our culture has changed dramatically in the past few years. Things once illegal are now lawful. Things once thought immoral are now acceptable at many levels. Things once viewed with a negative lens are now accepted and magnified in public light, even praised in some arenas.

This delusion of truth causes a further erosion of our moral fabric and makes it increasingly difficult to discern between right and wrong.

Whatever happened to standing up for right and speaking out for truth? What happened to courage and independence in the face of opposition, challenging the status quo when the status quo has left its foundation of principle? Who yet remains willing to go against the flow when the flow is fashionable and trendy?

The right path is not always the easiest nor the most popular.

As you navigate your path to *the other side*, you will encounter many struggles and obstacles. It is in those times more than ever that your commitment to the process and the charted course proves critical.

Consider the Salmon and Its Unique Life Cycle

The salmon run is a time when salmon, which have migrated from the ocean, swim to the upper reaches of rivers where they spawn on gravel beds. Salmon typically spend their early life in rivers, then swim out to sea where they live their adult lives and gain most of their body mass. Once they have matured, they return to the rivers to spawn. Usually, they return with uncanny precision to the natal river where they were born, and even to the very spawning ground of their birth.

> *The right path is not always the easiest nor the most popular.*

Some salmon are anadromous, a term which means *"running upward."* Anadromous fish grow up mostly in the saltwater in oceans. When they have matured, they migrate or *"run up"* freshwater rivers to spawn. They're actually born in freshwater, navigate to live in saltwater, then migrate back to freshwater. Their biomechanics change to allow this type of transition from freshwater to saltwater and back to freshwater again.

There are many obstacles to the run.

Salmon start the run in peak condition, the culmination of years of development in the ocean. They need high swimming and leaping abilities to battle the rapids and other obstacles the river may present. All their energy goes into the physical rigors of the journey and the dramatic transition they must still complete before they are ready for the spawning events ahead.

The run up river will be exhausting, sometimes requiring the salmon to battle hundreds of miles upstream against strong currents and a myriad of formidable enemies hindering their path. Chinook and sockeye salmon from central Idaho must travel some 900 miles and climb nearly 7,000 feet in elevation before they are ready to spawn.

Salmon are also required to negotiate waterfalls, rapids and other obstacles by leaping or jumping. They have been recorded making vertical jumps as high as 12 feet.

Consider, if God put such a definitive compass and robust drive in a fish, isn't it easier to believe He also put something in man that would allow him to make significant personal changes and complete near fatal exploits? Likewise, isn't it easier to believe man could also make abnormal strides in areas that otherwise seem impossible, like reaching *the other side*?

I believe we can do things that are far from what society calls normal. In this, I believe we can accomplish great feats and overcome tremendous obstacles if we are willing to put forth the effort.

Remember, Jesus said, *"All things are possible if we believe."* [45]

Establishing the possibility, there are certain parameters that must be met in order to do the impossible. Obviously, faith is critical to the equation. If you don't believe it's possible, how can you ever expect it to happen?

Second, we must have an appropriate response that works hand in hand with our faith. James 2:20 says, *"Faith without works is dead."* [46] One translation says, *"Without corresponding action, faith is lifeless."*

In my opinion, this is where many people fall short when trying to reach *the other side.* We've been through hell and found a way to survive. We've managed to find hope and a stronger faith. At last, when it's time to put legs to our aspirations; those "corresponding actions" often fail to accompany our faith. Unless we incorporate daily decisions and activities that lead us along the correct or corrected path, we will continue to struggle.

This takes a great commitment. An "all or nothing" mind-set. An "in it to win it" mentality. Much like the salmon, swimming upstream, regardless of how difficult the journey may become, we must be committed to the end. There can be nothing in us that gives in to the possibility of turning around when things get hard. Every single day we must give our very best effort.

After Tammye and I received our rhema word about *the other side,* we still had to negotiate some very arduous and exhausting situations.

We had to learn how to communicate differently. We had to adjust to living under the same roof again.

We had to adjust our lifestyles to reflect our union. We weren't separated any longer and that meant changes to our daily routines.

We were forced to make major decisions regarding our finances. We now had a considerable amount of personal debt that had accumulated during the dark days. Debt that threatened to take what was left of our life's work.

Our home, land, vehicles, jewelry, tools and toys; as well as, everything else we had managed to amass over twenty plus years, were all vulnerable and at risk. Even on the brightest days, bankruptcy often seemed to be the best choice. Thankfully, we were able to avoid this option, even though numerous attorneys and financial strategists advised this was the only way out.

We had to learn how to control our emotions differently. We had to learn how to deal with painful and debilitating feelings that continually wanted to rear their ugly heads.

We fully recognized that many things had to change, or else we would end up in the same dilemma. As the saying goes, *"If you do what you've always done, you'll get what you've always had. If you want what you've never had, you have to do what you've never done."*

> *"If you do what you've always done, you'll get what you've always had. If you want what you've never had, you have to do what you've never done.*

It was not easy. It was painfully difficult. At times, it seemed completely impossible. Sadly, there were very few people encouraging us to try. Most felt it would be better for us to give up and start over with someone else. I will admit, there were times we wondered if they were right.

It was crazy how many *"little things"* could throw off the balance of an otherwise peaceful day. The tone of a ringing cell phone. An item on the menu at your favorite restaurant. A vehicle passing on the highway. A television show or song on the radio. The list goes on and on and on.

At times, we felt like the proverbial bull in a china closet. Our struggles were so overwhelming; yet, our steps required the intimate balance and fragile coercion of a ballerina on Broadway.

We absolutely had to tiptoe through a number of delicate situations, where our emotions were screaming as loud as they possibly could. Taking a deep breath and a short walk were never far from consideration. The emotional stresses of rebuilding our family were substantially more than we ever imagined.

The challenges far exceeded any physical dilemma, partly due to the fact that our minds are incapable of differentiating between fact or fiction, today or yesterday, real or fantasy. Every activity in our life is accompanied by a wide array of emotions. Those emotions come flooding back when that memory is recalled.

Unfortunately, we don't always control when a memory is recalled. Likewise, relative emotions may decide to chaperone the moment, with or without our permission. It is difficult, at best, to control these emotions. Even more so, the often awkward timing at which they make their presence known. We can, however, control what we do with them and how we address the moment of their appearance.

The subtlest thing can trigger a memory and the emotions that accompany it.

Think about your first kiss or the birth of your child. All the wonderful emotions that accompany that specific memory arrive instantly. Consider your worst nightmare or a terrible argument. Suddenly, your blood pressure is on the rise and you're ready to fight.

> *The subtlest thing can trigger a memory and the emotions that accompany it.*

This is the nature of our emotions. Our mind has incredible properties and when used to our advantage can bring substantial benefits. If left unchecked, our emotions can wreak havoc on an otherwise harmonious afternoon.

James 1:21 says to *"receive with meekness the engrafted word, which is able to <u>save your souls</u>."*[47]

This verse is not talking about salvation, as in the new birth. It is partly addressing the stability of our emotions, as our intellect and emotions are connected to our soul. Many people, even born-again, Spirit-filled believers, often have difficulty with their emotions. Up today and down tomorrow. Happy for a bit, then sad. It's as if they're on a roller-coaster ride of emotions.

As we allow the Word to be implanted into our spirit man, we should become more stable in every area of life, including our emotions. Feeding our spirit man with healthy, Word-based, life-giving material will eradicate emotional, spiritual and physical strongholds.

I've often asked, "If you have two dogs in a fight, which one will win the fight?" The answer is actually quite simple. The dog you feed the most will win. If you feed your spirit man, he will win the fight for dominance in your life. Feed him Word-based truth, and he will lead you into prosperity, health and a fulfilling life of happiness.

To the contrary, if we allow our emotions to feed on anything that presents itself as a nutritional convenience, we may find a constant diet of unhealthy, ungodly ideas searching for a place to call home.

We will never arrive at a place of strength and balance unless we partake of the things that yield such a life. We tell our children, *"You are what you eat."* Likewise, this truth avails itself beyond the physical bread and into the spiritual and emotional pantries of our home. This is one paradigm that never changes regardless of age, race, religious preferences or family creed.

> *Emotional stability is a sign of spiritual maturity.*

Emotional stability is a sign of spiritual maturity.

Emotional instability creates incredible hardships on a relationship, even more so when trying to rebuild. When we're already frustrated, tired and stretched to our limit, we can ill afford to allow our emotions to add insult to injury.

We are expecting our partner to change, grow up and act like an adult. Thus, we need to expect the same of ourselves, holding to the highest degree of excellence and maturity, regardless of emotional influence.

This can be incredibly difficult when our emotions want to control us. If we are going to reach *the other side*, we will need to exercise jurisdiction over this area.

You cannot allow emotions to dictate your life.

Remember Jesus and His disciples on the ship when the storm was raging? The disciples were all wound up in fear and emotions; justifiably so, some would argue. On the other hand, Jesus was asleep, at peace. It was a distinct difference in emotional stability or instability depending on your perspective. It was also a notable difference in maturity.

> ✌
> *You cannot allow emotions to dictate your life.*

Jesus didn't get emotional about the storm. He remained calm and took actions that corresponded to His faith. He *"spoke"* to the wind and the sea. He didn't scream at the wind nor at the disciples who had awakened Him from His rest.

The enemy will do everything within its power to move us into the arena of emotion and reason. If we allow ourselves to reside in this place, we will struggle on many fronts. Our victory is not based on emotions. It is not based on reason. It is based on faith in God, accompanied by a determined Word-based path of resolution.

The enemy wants to derail our efforts by causing us to lose our temper. It wants us to get all excited and start running off at the mouth. It wants us to lose control and say or do something we'll regret later. That's the enemy's plan.

We absolutely cannot give in to this ploy. If we are truly committed to reaching *the other side*, we must take the necessary measures to ensure our stability, thus creating an environment conducive to success.

If we have anger issues, we need to engage in the appropriate measures to learn how to control that emotion. If we have problems with lust, set boundaries that ensure lust can no longer influence our decisions.

If we have relationships that continually cause disruptions, we may need to let them go and establish new relationships. If the wrong person is always trying to call or text us, we should either block their number or get a whole new number ourself; **and then don't give it out** to the free world.

If our current job is causing problems, we should consider changing jobs or even starting a new career. *It's better to be jobless and have a happy family, than to own the company and live in hell.*

It may ultimately be necessary to completely relocate to another city, change addresses, change churches, change our favorite restaurant, change grocery stores and even change where we get our morning coffee. We must do whatever is necessary in order to create a climate conducive to success; as well as, establishing appropriate boundaries that protect us from further chaos. We cannot allow anything nor anyone to rob us of the opportunity to make it to *the other side*.

Being fully committed requires us to put everything on the table and evaluate it openly. Nothing, and I do mean nothing, can be eliminated from this survey. We must look close and hard at everything and everyone in our life. We must be willing to uproot, dislodge, redirect, modify, restructure and revamp any part of our life necessary to help us find the peace we have so adamantly pursued. We must refuse to allow anything or anyone to hold us back.

This is the type of commitment required when we're swimming upstream. Salmon never gather with their friends-in-fins to search for an easier path. It's already programmed into their DNA the route they will navigate. They don't even consider it difficult. They simply consider it an acceptable stipulation if they are to succeed in repopulating their species.

> *Being fully committed requires us to put everything on the table and evaluate it openly.*

Tammye and I made drastic changes, some of which were very painful. We agreed that everything was in play, and nothing was out of bounds except our faith. We recognized it was absolutely necessary to evaluate every influence if we were going to have any chance of rebuilding our family.

The purpose of our journey cannot be questioned. Likewise, we must make it clear to all who are in our circle, they will not be allowed to influence our decisions any longer. This is our journey, not theirs!

Our commitment must be unequaled. Our focus undistracted. Our determination unparalleled.

Commitment is NOT free and it's never easy.

It's not a casual desire. It's not a shallow New Year's resolution. It's not a Facebook challenge. It's a life-altering, meaningful, heartfelt, deep down devotion.

No doubt we've all heard about the farm animals wanting to make breakfast for the farmer on his birthday. The chicken said, "I'll give eggs." The cow said, "I'll give milk and butter." The pig said, "Wait just a minute! You fellows are only making a donation, but you're asking me to make a real commitment."

> ❧
>
> *Ask yourself, "Is my commitment strong enough to get me to the other side?"*

A true commitment is not cheap. It's not easy. It's a choice that will set the course for our life.

Ask yourself, *"Is my commitment strong enough to get me to the other side?"* If it isn't, you will most likely never make it. Stop playing games. Get serious about it and do what you know needs to be done.

Yes, it will be hard and may get even harder, but this is your life. Put forth the effort required to make it the best life possible. In the end, you'll be happier, more at peace and more thankful. Overall, you'll be a better person. Your family will appreciate this. Your friends will admire it. Most of all, you'll live the satisfaction of knowing you didn't give up.

Chapter 26

The Purple Flower

Everyone faces problems at one time or another. Dilemmas are a bit like busses. If you miss one, there'll be another along in a few minutes. Whether you're young or old, tall or short, rich or poor, you will face your fair share of challenges.

The crucial mark is how you approach problem solving with these challenges. There's an expression we used around the shop when we were working on our race cars. "Hit it with a hammer. If that doesn't work, use a bigger hammer."

Sadly, this is the most common way people go about solving problems. Blunt force, like a bull in a china shop. This is NOT the best way to solve problems.

Solving problems typically comes down to a few simple steps: evaluate the problem, find a solution and implement the process.

Obviously, we can elaborate in depth on each of these steps; but in the end, the approach is generally the same.

Solving problems typically comes down to a few simple steps: evaluate the problem, find a solution and implement the process.

I find it both frustrating and disappointing how many people choose not to follow the necessary procedures to solve their problems. The consensus in today's world is to quit, then start all over tomorrow with someone or something new and different.

Over the years, I've spoken to thousands of individuals who have gone through divorce, bankruptcy and other life-altering challenges. I always ask, "If given the chance, would you have done anything different in the way you handled that situation?" One hundred percent of the time, the answer has been unequivocally *"YES!"*

I understand there are individuals and situations in which that may not hold true, but for the thousands that I have spoken with over the past thirty years, *all* have said they would have approached those challenging times differently.

Imagine what would happen if we could reset thirty years of broken marriages, disrupted lives and defunct businesses. I'm confident our communities would look entirely different. Imagine what would happen if you could reset the last season of your life. If you're anything like most, myself included, you too would do a few things differently.

In the same regard, I've counseled and worked with thousands of individuals in the criminal justice system. From sex offenders and murderers, to petty thieves and users, I've asked the same question: "If given the chance, would you have done anything differently?" Once again, 100 percent of the time the answer has been an absolute *"YES!"*

As they say, hindsight is 20/20; but just imagine how many lives would have taken a different path and how much destruction and pain could have been eliminated if someone had taken the time to find the right solution for their dilemma.

Rather than looking back, let's focus our attention on the present and the future. Will we continue to use antiquated techniques to resolve futuristic dilemmas? Will we continue to offer outdated answers to new and unresolved problems?

What will we do differently today that we didn't do yesterday?

It was once believed that man couldn't fly. The Wright brothers were determined to bring new revelation to that paradigm. Electricity, the telephone, cars, computers, the Internet and so on. For thousands of years, man has been reaching for new plateaus in solving everyday problems.

> *What will we do differently today that we didn't do yesterday?*

What if we could jump forward in time a hundred years or so and take a look at things? How many of today's problems would have been solved and become of little significance? Would world hunger still exist? What about terminal illness, poverty, illiteracy and so many other elements that are substantial matters of concern for our generation?

I believe many of these matters will be resolved in the future. I can say that with a degree of certainty, because we can look back a hundred years and see how far we've come.

It's been said that the twentieth century brought the most advances ever in the history of man. Wouldn't it be interesting if we could look into the twenty-fifth century and see how many of those advances had become obsolete?

It's easy to get frustrated and feel like there's nothing we can do in the face of problems. Understand this, our "present" inability to recognize a solution is not an absolute indication that the answer doesn't exist. There is an answer. We just need to find it.

There are answers to every problem we are facing today.

When I was in Junior High School, our class went on a field trip. While riding the bus home that evening, one of the sponsors told a story that I've never forgotten. It captivated me for what seemed like an eternity.

> ❧
>
> *There are answers to every problem we are facing today.*

As the story went, a man was searching for the answer to an important question about life. He searched high and low. Every person he spoke with seemed to tell him the same thing, "When you find the illusive purple flower, you'll find your answer."

Days turned to weeks. Weeks turned to months. Before he knew it, he had been searching for the mystical purple flower for more than fifty years. He had trekked to the Himalayas to speak with Tibetan monks. He had journeyed to the poles of the earth, through the deserts and jungles, across great mountains and navigated the seven seas. Still, no purple flower.

One day, while searching the ancient archives in the basement of the Smithsonian, he made an unbelievable discovery. There it was, right before his eyes. The answer he had spent a lifetime searching for.

With tears falling on his cheeks and joy bursting from his soul, he leaped to his feet and began to scream, "I've found it! I've finally found it! After all these years, I've found the answer! The illusive purple flower has finally revealed its hidden treasure."

As he ran through the library, out the front door, down the steps and into the street, suddenly a horrific event occurred. He was so excited after all those years to find the answer, so distracted by his revelation, he ran out in front of an oncoming bus. Instantly, he was taken into eternity, carrying with him the long-sought secret of the illusive purple flower.

I remember riding on that bus, hearing this long, drawn-out story, thinking to myself, *"What was the secret? What did he find? Tell me!"*

With a smile and a bit of cynicism, the sponsor calmly explained the moral of the story: *"Always look both ways before crossing the street."*

The true moral of the story is to never give up searching for the answer. Regardless of how difficult it may be to find, keep looking until you find it. Why trade a lifetime of happiness simply because the answer to a difficult problem was illusive?

Remember Solomon, the man we mentioned earlier? For thousands of years, he has been recognized as the wisest man who ever lived. According to the Bible, God came to him and asked him what he wanted. "Whatever it is, I'll give it to you."

He could've asked for money, power, honor or any other of a million things you and I can think of. Instead, he asked for wisdom and knowledge that would help him be a more effective leader as he searched for solutions to the problems of his people. In response, God granted his request and gave him wealth, possessions and honor as well.

> *Why trade a lifetime of happiness simply because the answer to a difficult problem was illusive?*

In the book of Proverbs, Solomon speaks a great deal about wisdom, knowledge and understanding. He says, "Fools despise wisdom and knowledge." He instructs his son, "Turn your ear to wisdom and apply your heart to understanding." He encourages us to search for it as if we are searching for "hidden treasure" much like searching for silver or precious jewels.

Most people struggle to read a helpful book, attend counseling more than a few times or make any significant changes to help resolve their conflict. Yet Solomon, the man of great godly wisdom, says you have to search hard for the answers to life's most difficult questions.

Rest assured, reaching *the other side* is not easy. It's highly possible, but rarely easy.

You must commit everything within your power to finding the appropriate solution to your problem.

I once heard a story about a young man who journeyed far and near searching for answers. Along the way, he encountered a host of friends who each gave him a precious gem, a nugget of truth, which he carried with him. Toward the end of the journey, he realized that he had amassed a wealth of precious gems. Each gem represented a great truth.

> *You must commit everything within your power to finding the appropriate solution to your problem.*

The answer wasn't at the end of his journey. Rather, it was given to him a fragment at a time, all along the way. Had he given up, he would most certainly have missed his destiny.

No doubt you've heard the expression, "Life is a journey, not a destination." The same is true for *the other side*. Regardless of when and where you arrive, a new set of challenges will always be waiting.

Once you understand the process and grasp the concept, you will never again be afraid to face any problem. Your level of maturity and understanding will be enhanced and will lift you to new heights of living.

Spilled milk is a great crisis for a three year old. It should not be the same for a person of thirty. Likewise, the more you live and the more you discover those precious gems of wisdom, the more likely you are to rise above the conflicts. *The other side* should not be a once-in-a-lifetime journey; rather, it should be a mind-set you embrace every day.

Chapter 27

Baseball, Batman & Brothers

Before I tell you how our story turns out, I'd like to take you back a few years, back to my childhood. Understanding where we came from can be helpful in getting where we want to go.

Growing up in a small Midwest town, life was simple. Nothing too complicated. Nothing too overwhelming, or so it seemed to me. Everyone knew everyone. Life was about God, country and family. There were no video games, no cell phones, no Internet. There was a pinball game at the skating rink, but that cost money and money wasn't free.

Today, some might think it was a boring life, but quite the contrary. It was a great life. After school, boys would gather in our backyard and play Wiffle ball (plastic ball and bat). Usually, the ball would get cracked, so we would tape it up with some of Dad's black electrical tape.

Man oh man, did we ever have some great games. Wiffle ball could be very intense, especially for a group of young boys. Tempers flared, dirt flew and always . . . someone would be accused of cheating. For some reason, my brother was usually the one being accused. I'm not saying he did anything wrong, but questions are still unanswered to this day.

No one could play Wiffle ball like my older brother. He was the greatest of the greats. When he pitched, he could make the ball do things that no one else could ever do. It was like that little plastic (taped up) ball had eyes and special wings. It would move around so much it was almost impossible to hit. That was our life, and life was good.

Every day the boys would come around and get up a game. The world series of Wiffle ball was right there in our backyard. It didn't matter if it was hot or cold, rain or shine, we played ball. That is, until Batman came on TV at 4:00. The game would have to wait to see if the caped crusaders could miraculously escape the villain's evil trap.

Those were some great times. Dirty faces, skinned knees, Wiffle ball and Batman. How could life get any better? At school we talked and bragged about who won yesterday's game or how many home runs we hit. As always, there was chitchat about my brother cheating; then more chatter about whether or not Batman and Robin would escape. After school, it was back to the games.

> *Never underestimate the value of friendship.*

We bonded as close friends. Many of those friendships are still strong to this day, more than forty years later. It's amazing what can come of good friends.

Never underestimate the value of friendship.

Your friends may someday be the difference in your life. True friends are hard to find and even harder to convince that everything in your life is all right, especially when it's not. Real friends are a compliment to your dreams and help you find the strength and courage to do the impossible. A friend is still there to help you when everyone else is gone. A friend is the one picking you up after you've fallen flat on your face. Scripture says, *"As iron sharpens iron, so a man sharpens the countenance of his friend."*[48]

There were several sets of brothers in our group. They were the same boys hunting and fishing in some of those earlier stories. My brother and I, much like the other sets of brothers, were almost three years apart. Just the right gap to still be friends, even though we were brothers.

If you were blessed like me to have an older brother, then you understand. You were allowed to call each other ugly, embarrassing names; throw rocks at each other; shoot at each other with BB guns and bottle rockets, and of course, tell on them when they were cheating in the ball game.

It was a special bond. It's called brotherhood. Regardless of how mean you might be to each other or how much you said you hated each other, the truth was, your brother was probably the greatest guy in the whole wide world. At least, that's the way I felt. It was okay for us to fight each other, but you need to keep your nose out of our business or we'll both turn on you.

I didn't have to worry about getting beat up by some smart aleck bully. I had a big brother who would take care of it. I always knew he was watching over me, even when I couldn't see him. (Some things never change, thankfully.)

Our little band of misfits, the brotherhood from which Wiffle ball legends were made, had some interesting times over the years. We were always together playing ball, going fishing, riding bicycles and whatever else we could find to do that didn't cost money. Some days, it seems like a lifetime ago. At other times, it seems like it was only yesterday.

To this day, I'm still immensely thankful for those boys and our times together. I was always the youngest, the smallest and the runt; but I felt safe. I never worried about anything happening to me or anyone picking on me. After all, the greatest Wiffle ball pitcher of all time, aka my big brother, would be there to help if ever I needed him. I was also confident in my friends' ability to help protect me from anything or anyone trying to hurt me.

Do you have someone in your life that you can count on to help in your darkest night? It may not be your biological sibling, but a "brother" or "sister" just the same. Someone you can talk to openly with the confidence that no one will ever know what you discussed? Someone who understands you, gets you, knows all your secrets; yet, for unknown reasons, still stands beside you?

As we engage in analysis and anecdote, let me also encourage you to have at least one good friend by your side. Someone you can trust with any area of your life, including your family. Someone who is not trying to gain anything from your moment of need. Someone who actually helps you rather than complicates your life with more chaos.

I'm not talking about a drinking buddy or a girlfriend to shop with. I'm talking about someone of substantial integrity. An accountability partner. Someone capable of keeping private matters private. Someone willing to call you out when you're off course. Someone strong enough to help keep you together when you feel like falling apart.

It's not easy to find this type of friend. If you have someone like this, it's quite probable they've walked this tumultuous journey with you. More than likely, there have been a few days when they challenged the salt of your friendship by offering a helpful observation you didn't agree with. Maybe they simply served up the truth or brandished a resolve that no one else had the courage to offer.

When you make it to *the other side,* don't forget to thank your truest friends, the ones that refused to abandon you in your greatest despair. I have several friends like this. I will forever cherish the authenticity of our relationships. I am forever indebted to them and will never forget their contribution to my family's destiny.

I'd also like to introduce you to the greatest Friend you could ever know. With His assistance, your journey will find strength you never imagined; hope you presumed was lost; and peace no one else will understand.

He is a Friend who sticks closer than a brother. He is the sunrise to your darkest night. The surgeon who cures the incurable. The counselor with a creative solution. The safe harbor from every storm.

He will not leave you when others forsake you. He will not belittle you when others mock you. He will not condemn you when the whole world passes judgment.

He will love you unconditionally, forgive you uncharacteristically, embrace you eternally and support you every step of the way.

He is not mad at you. He is not angry with you. He is not disappointed with you.

He believes in you like no other and has great plans for you. Regardless of anything else you may have believed or been taught, this truth must be alive in your heart.

You will have ample opportunities to question His involvement in your life. You may even feel tempted to blame Him for your sorrows.

Settle it now, He is your Friend, and He is here to help you get to *the other side.* His name is Jesus Christ.

I encourage you to simply bow your head and ask Him to help you. It's extremely simple. You might say, *"Dear Jesus, I ask You to help me. Come into my heart. Guide me to a place of peace and comfort. Give me the strength and courage to face the challenges that are before me. I put my trust in You. Amen."*

Chapter 28

Bullfrogs and Butterflies

When I was about eight years old, I found something quite amazing. While playing in the yard, I found an odd object attached to a small tree limb. I wasn't sure what it was, so I took the small limb, with the object attached, and presented it to Mom.

"It's a cocoon," she said. *"In a few days, a butterfly will come out of it."*

I was too young to know much about science and nature, but I was certainly ready to learn about this. I took the small branch, with the cocoon attached, and placed it inside a clear plastic bag (with air holes); then hung it on our back porch. The porch was closed in, so it was out of the elements. More importantly, it gave me an opportunity for a close-up view of what was about to transpire.

Every day for about a week, I monitored that little cocoon. Sure enough, just as Mom had predicted, a beautiful butterfly soon emerged from that little odd shaped object. I could hardly believe my eyes. It was so beautiful, so graceful.

When I opened the bag to let it fly away, it didn't. It fluttered around, gently floating on every breath of sunshine. It seemed to embrace its newfound freedom in a grace that couldn't be explained. Yet, for some unknown reason, it stayed close to wherever I was. At the end of the day, I gently placed it back in the clear plastic bag (with air holes). It wasn't the perfect place to keep a pet butterfly, but at least it provided a temporary home that night.

The next day I decided to take my butterfly to school with me. I was the coolest kid in class that day. I was the only kid in school who had a pet butterfly.

Everywhere I went that day, my butterfly clung to me. To this day, I can't explain how or why, but it did happen just as I'm describing. It would flutter off for a bit, then return right back to me. It stayed attached to my shirt as I walked to school and then when I walked home. It would dance around in the spring air, then come right back to me.

I felt somehow responsible for it as if I needed to take care of it. I didn't know what to do nor how to take care of a butterfly, so I tried to be as caring and gentle as possible. The one thing I did know about butterflies is that they are not only beautiful and graceful, they are also extremely fragile. By the end of the day, it decided to float off to wherever butterflies go at night.

As I began to learn about the process of metamorphosis, I quickly learned that the caterpillar had to go through a delicate but significant change. Not only was its entire countenance different, so too was part of its molecular structure.

In as much, I also learned that bullfrogs go through a similar metamorphic transition, changing from tadpoles to bullfrogs. There are many similarities in the concept of metamorphosis, yet the obvious differences between bullfrogs and butterflies go without mention.

There are some Eastern religions that believe humans migrate through various stages of metamorphosis, passing from one physical form to another; through the transition of death and then a rebirth.

I can't say that I agree with this belief system; however, I do believe we go through transitions as we navigate through life. The metamorphosis may not be as significant as that of the bullfrog or butterfly, and certainly not changing physical forms into a completely different earthbound existence. But change certainly reaches into every life.

There is little doubt that life's greatest storms have an effect on us that bring about change.

The effect can be slight or significant, but there will be a transition from the storms of today that help shape who we are tomorrow.

Soldiers returning from war often have difficulty fitting back into the routine life they once lived. The atrocities experienced on the battlefield can leave proportionate imbalances, both mentally and emotionally, not to mention the physical scars which often result from a combat encounter. This change can bring about noticeable differences in a person, so much that strategic counseling programs are necessary to help soldiers cope with the transitions of returning home after being deployed.

> *There is little doubt that life's greatest storms have an effect on us that bring about change.*

Those who have faced life-threatening or life-altering events often exhibit paramount changes in their personality. A once hardened, calloused individual may emerge from one of these events or seasons as soft-hearted, thankful and emotional. Just the same, a once lighthearted, easy going person may emerge as bitter and angry.

The death of a loved one, a broken marriage or a failed business all bring about change to those who experience the moment.

It can be difficult to predict the specific outcome a person may represent, except to say they will most certainly be different. Hopefully, a realization of what truly matters in life will bring clarity and focus over the clutter of life's chaos.

> ❧
>
> *I can say without question that I am different as a result of the storms in my life.*

I can say without question that I am different as a result of the storms in my life. To be completely honest, I feel I have changed in both good and bad ways.

There are days when I find myself being more cynical and less patient with individuals who do not have my best interests at heart. At the same time, I am more understanding, patient and compassionate for those who are hurting and in need of help.

It's difficult to explain; almost like I am both a bullfrog and a butterfly at the same time.

Some things seem to have no impact on me whatsoever. Yet, an untimely song on the radio or scene in a movie can bring an uncomfortable influence that drives me to a lonely place of pain and regret. Irritation can arrive on a whim, yet peace often exhibits itself in situations I previously couldn't manage.

I believe, in most ways, I have emerged as a better individual. Still, there are days when I wonder who I am. I still struggle at times with the new me. I give great attention to my purpose, my thoughts, words and movements. Prayerfully, I will someday be completely relieved of the anxiety and inharmonious residue left from the storm.

It should be our goal to take everything we've learned from the storms, and use those insights as motivation to help change us for the better. Stronger. Healthier. Happier. We should work to take the negative energy of the storm and harness its power to propel us forward as if we are a ship at sea, embracing the winds of adversity—allowing them to fill our sails and breathe life into our destiny.

> *We should work to take the negative energy of the storm and harness its power to propel us forward.*

The choice lies within each of us how we let the storms affect us. We can view ourselves as either a victim or a victor, subsequently defining our new persona.

If I have any desire to help strengthen those closest to me, I need first to make sure I have the necessary strength and perspective to affect such change.

It's okay to change. It's acceptable to transform, especially when the new you has discernible differences capable of mitigating life's challenges in ways never before embraced in your life.

The bullfrog and butterfly never fight against the transition. They simply acknowledge the inevitable and surrender themselves to the best future possible. In as much, they recognize that certain changes to their lifestyle must also encompass their new look.

The bullfrog loses its tail and grows legs. The butterfly no longer crawls around, but asserts its grace as it flutters from flower to flower. This should be the new you—graceful and intentional, moving with passion and purpose as you explore a new paradigm.

> ❧
>
> *You are not the same person who entered the storm. You are different now.*

You are not the same person who entered the storm. You are different now.

I realize the storm may have taken its toll on you. It may have hit you like a hurricane. Still, you have a choice of how you come out on *the other side.* It doesn't matter if you're a bullfrog or a butterfly; determine to be the best version of you possible.

Chapter 29

A Great Place to Call Home

In Genesis, the Bible speaks of a place called the Garden of Eden. It's where Adam and Eve lived. It was a place many believe God created just for them. A place of great beauty and abundance. A place where His presence was exhibited on a continual basis. A place where it was common to walk with Him, face to face.

Scripture identifies the Garden as a place of bountiful resources. An opulent oasis full of rich mineral deposits. A place with an overabundance of food and plant life. A picture of perfection. A sanctuary of plentitude. It was devoid of evil, sin and sickness and a great place to call home.

Have you ever stopped to consider what happened to the Garden of Eden?

Over the centuries, many have raised this very question. Numerous archeologists, explorers and theologians have attempted to establish its exact location, but all have come to the same fruitless end.

> *Have you ever stopped to consider what happened to the Garden of Eden?*

One would think, or hope, identifying its location is within our grasp, especially considering the incredible technologies and advanced science available in today's world.

In a 1999 article, John D. Morris, Ph.D., President of the Institute for Creation Research cites:

"Over the years, many have claimed the Garden of Eden has been found. Of course, the location of each 'discovery' is in a different location. The Bible describes the area around the Garden in Genesis 2, even using recognizable place names such as Ethiopia. It mentions a spring in the Garden which parts into four major rivers, including the Euphrates. This has led many, including Bible scholars, to conclude that the Garden of Eden was somewhere in the middle eastern area known today as the Tigris-Euphrates River Valley, with its remains long ago vanishing.

It is also true that this area (the "fertile crescent") was the location of the ancient Tower of Babel and the patriarch Abraham's home in the city of Ur. Without a doubt, the Tigris-Euphrates River Valley plays a unique role in biblical history, but was it the location of the Garden of Eden?"

There is an additional theory of the Garden's location. Some have proposed that even with particular landmarks being identified in Genesis, the exact location of the Garden may have moved around.

Proponents of this theory allege the Garden was wherever God's presence dwelt, citing the intimate, sin-free relationship that allowed man to live continually in God's presence, thus allowing Adam and Eve to live in the Garden. It is further speculated that the Garden was an earthly manifestation of His heavenly presence.

You will note in Genesis 3, it was the serpent of "the field" who tempted Eve. According to this account, the serpent lived in the field, but was apparently allowed access to the Garden. This would seem consistent with scripture found in Job, revealing Satan's access to God, in efforts to gain permission to tempt Job.

If this theory is too great a stretch on your theology, please be patient. I am merely presenting the possibilities of a mobile Garden and the likelihood that it represented more than just an oasis of opulence.

We are also not certain of the amount of time Adam and Eve lived in the Garden. We can only speculate. It is entirely possible, they could have lived there for several thousand years or maybe just a few days. What is not left for speculation is the truth that peace and abundance accompany God's presence and were readily available in the Garden of Genesis 2.

After the fall of man, we are taught that God's presence on earth dwelt in various mobile locations, such as the ark of the covenant which was typically kept in the Holy of Holies, inside the temple. In this scenario, the high priest was only allowed to enter the Holy of Holies once per year. On this occasion, he was required to first make the appropriate sacrifices to cleanse himself, thereby making it possible to be in God's presence.

The ark was associated with God's presence, thus bringing blessing, strength and abundance wherever the ark rested.

When Jesus walked the earth abundance, health, life, peace, joy and a constant display of God's presence accompanied Him wherever He went.

Jesus proclaimed God's presence would now be available to *all* men, not to simply abide *with* them but *in* them. This was a considerable claim.

At that time, the presence of God on earth was revealed in the ark and the temple. Furthermore, it was only conferred upon certain individuals, such as kings, priests and prophets. Jesus was all three—king, priest and prophet. It was written that He had the anointing, the presence of God, "without measure."

For all men to have access to God, anytime and anywhere, was a substantial change. At the time, it was considered heresy to even speak of something so preposterous. It was, however, part of the divine purpose for Jesus coming to earth, to restore man to his original position—just as he was in the Garden. This holds monumental importance, not only for Adam, but also for us. When God put man in the Garden, He accredited to him a position of righteousness, whereby man could stand in God's presence without any sense of guilt or shame. Through His sacrifice, Jesus made it possible for man to be restored to this righteous position.

This would allow mankind to once again have an intimate, sin-free relationship with God. In turn, this meant man could once again live in the promise of *zoe*, the God-kind of life.

Never more would man be required to offer the sacrifice of atonement. Once and for all, Christ had offered a sacrifice of redemption. Beyond this, the Holy Spirit was now given to reside both *with and inside* of every believer. The constant presence of God providing life, peace, comfort, health, direction, restoration and so much more was a return to the type of living Adam and Eve experienced in the Garden.

This is still a challenge for some to accept. Nonetheless, it is why Jesus came. If you're still not convinced, read the Gospel of John. Pay particular attention to all the times Jesus says He came to give us life (*zoe*).

We went through fire and flood, but you brought us to a place of great abundance (Psalm 66:12 NLT).

For Tammye and I, we felt like we had been through hell. In no way, shape or form were we living the zoe kind of life. It may have been available to us, but we weren't walking in it. Nothing about our living conditions resembled the Garden.

We could more closely relate to the part of this verse about going through fire and flood. We had been in a lengthy season of tribulation. A season of turmoil that nearly destroyed us and everything we placed value in, including our faith.

> ❧
>
> *We went through fire and flood, but you brought us to a place of great abundance (Psalm 66:12 NLT).*

If you've read this far, then you have a decent grasp of what we faced. If you just joined the story, here's the short version.

We nearly lost our marriage. We were embarrassed in our ministry. The IRS threatened devastating penalties in a targeted assault. We faced the daunting task of fending off bankruptcy. On most days, it was a challenge just to keep the utilities on. We were named in multiple lawsuits. Tammye endured several midlife career changes. I sustained a traumatic brain injury from a car accident; and these are just the highlights (or should I say *lowlights*).

It would be an understatement to say we struggled to find a sense of peace and purpose. More accurately, we had difficulty even finding a reason to live. Getting out of bed to start another day presented a tremendous challenge. Some described us as the perfect country song, a real mess.

Not to forget, our family also faced significant challenges. Austin was overrun by a semi-truck, while traveling home from Bible college. He too withstood the most difficult season of his young life, including major back surgery at just nineteen years of age.

Mom persevered through several life-threatening illnesses, all while Dad battled cancer and two major heart attacks.

Only by God's grace is our family healthy, whole and living an abundant life today.

This was definitely a season our entire family would like to forget. Though we would never be able to forget it, we were prayerful we would someday, somehow get beyond it.

When we first heard those words, *the other side*, we weren't exactly sure what they meant. What we did have was an intimate understanding that it was a place of peace, tranquility and God's blessing. A place where we could walk in His presence, knowing that He was with us.

For a handful of years, we struggled to find our place and restore our family. Time after time, we discussed *the other side*. It was one of the promises we held onto, but for the most part, it was just a dream of a far and distant land.

We often remarked, "Someday this will all be behind us. Someday we will reach *the other side*." We recognized, at some point, our hope in *someday* would have to turn to faith in *this day*. Eventually, through hard work, faith and patience, our "someday" arrived.

Some might say our ship had come in. For us, it was more akin to a repurposed life raft. It still wasn't much, but it was more than we had before. To our relief, the storm no longer raged and dry land was now on the horizon.

We were finally able to have those delicate conversations about painful areas of our life. At last we were able to navigate those formidable tempests and not fear our demise. Cautiously, we were even able to begin sharing parts of our story with others who were experiencing their own storm.

Little by little, our marriage was getting stronger. The sun had once again risen from a nighttime of torment. The storm had finally calmed and we had found a great place to call home.

Looking back, it's captivating to see all the good that came out of our season of peril.

During our season of futility, we managed to redefine our identities and establish opportunities whereby others could reach *the other side* of their calamity.

One such effort was a rebranding of our ministry. Our church had previously been named Christ Church. After that serendipitous trip where we received our enlightenment, we decided to realign our ministry and rename the church. It would now be called The Bridge at Christ Church.

> *Looking back, it's captivating to see all the good that came out of our season of peril.*

As we remembered our beginning, we made a conscious effort to focus our sights on helping the hurting and hopeless. Once again, we chose to reach out to others who were experiencing the same type of dilemma we had just gone through. We felt it was important to revisit our original vision and refresh its importance to our congregation.

A bridge was significant in this matter. After all, a bridge will connect you to *the other side.* (www.thebridgeatcc.org)

Today the church is vibrant and thriving. Every day ministry opportunities allow us to reach out to help those in need. Many of these people remind us of ourselves struggling, hurting and afraid of what may happen next.

In the process of rebuilding our lives, we found it helpful to take trips periodically. Sometimes it was just a couple hours down the road for a weekend getaway. When we could manage, we would go a little further.

Our first major trip after Tammye moved home was to the beautiful island of St. Croix. Strategically placed, our secluded cottage on the beach had no cell phone service and no Internet. This was perfect in that it eliminated any outside interference in our goal of reconnecting with each other.

A book, the beach, an exquisite sunset and a very fragile hand to hold. We rented a Jeep, traversed the island and found ways to enjoy just being alive. I can't begin to tell you how many conversations we had about *the other side*.

One day we decided to take a hike through the rainforest, along a mountain trail. We hoped to end up on a hidden beach. However, along the way, the marked path seemed to vanish and we found ourselves questioning our next steps. It seemed a bit symbolic, considering we had been lost for such a long time. But eventually, we did find our way in both regards.

One afternoon we made our way to the eastern most point of the island. We did something dramatic and difficult, yet we believed it would also be liberating and fruitful.

As we made our way along the jagged rocks, we forged ahead to a desolate shoreline where the surf was violently asserting its presence. It was there we managed the courage to stand up to our storm and command its calm.

Delicately and decisively, we each wrote on a separate piece of paper the things we most wanted to forget and the things for which we desired to receive forgiveness. We wrote of the nightmares that threatened to haunt us to our graves. Painfully, we noted the horrors pledging to torment us for all eternity.

Then and there, we placed the pieces of paper in a bottle. As I took Tammye in my arms, we embraced in prayer. *"Dear God, we ask You to forgive us of our indiscretions. Cleanse us of the evil that polluted our souls and somehow restore peace in our home. Help us find that special place You told us about."*

As our tears encouraged the ocean's tide, we threw that bottle as far as humanly possible. We pledged its contents only for the eyes of our Heavenly Father. We trusted in Him and the ocean's current that we would never see the bottle nor its contents again.

Only a season before, the sea of life had erupted in violence and hostility, yielding up the greatest storm we had ever experienced. Now, it was our turn to give back the horror and hell we never intended to own.

Slowly but surely that little bottle found its way in a new direction. A one-way voyage away from the shore and away from us. So, too, its cargo of vile memories destined to abandon our world. Its new home would be the dark abyss. Not even Jonah's great fish would be able to return that burden.

We held to Micah 7:19 NKJV which says, *"You will cast all our sins into the depths of the sea."* That was one parcel of our past we hoped to never see again. If God was willing to bury our sins in the sea, we were obliged to help.

For those who yearn for the hideous and horrific details of our journey, you will only find them in that bottle. They are forever removed from record in God's eyes. Likewise, it is our firm consensus to neither glamorize the failures nor resurrect the pain of that disastrous season.

I once heard a quote given to the credit of Corrie ten Boom: "If God chose to cast our sins into the depths of the sea, we shouldn't go fishing for them."

Vacations with PURPOSE

From that time till now, we attempt a get-a-way at least once every three or four months. On several occasions, we bought tickets and paid for our little excursion on a credit card. This strategy may not win the approval of financial wizards, but in our minds it was just another part of our therapy. It helped our relationship, so we were willing to invest.

We decided to call these little excursions "vacations with purpose." Each trip, we vowed to search out opportunities to assist or encourage someone along the way. Someone who might be facing the same dilemma as us.

Interestingly, it was these "vacations with purpose" that challenged us to launch a new endeavor called Project Dream Seeds. It is a non-profit humanitarian initiative, designed to plant seeds of hope in the lives of underserved children through food, water and education.

Today, significant efforts are made around the world to assist children and their families, and help them navigate the difficult waters of their own storm. We love to share stories of faith, encouraging these children to dream. We tell them they can be anything they choose: a doctor, lawyer, airplane pilot, fireman, teacher or preacher.

We challenge them to adopt our family creed: *Dream, Dream Big, Dream Often.* www.projectdreamseeds.org

In the fall of 2015, we were able to witness one of those dreams come to fruition as we launched another effort at helping those in need, Premier USA, Inc., a staffing and consulting business.

Once again, our goal was to assist families in crisis. We see value in helping a person find gainful employment, as we understand the strain placed on a family struggling to make ends meet. We recognize our involvement in helping them reach *the other side* of their peril as an opportunity to give back.

We embrace the occasion to offer our insights to businesses and ministries, both large and small, helping them achieve a mark of success.

It was a short journey to a very successful company, and it quickly marked the way for additional business endeavors. Without reserve, we've dedicated it to the service of God, establishing scholarships and various support systems in multiple communities. We have been privileged to partner with numerous international businesses, community groups and service organizations; and we believe a harvest of hope is entirely possible. www.premierusajobs.com

I could dedicate multiple pages talking about the many success stories we've encountered in recent days.

Some might think *the other side* is about driving luxury cars, living in palatial estates, traveling to exotic locations and having dinner in the finest restaurants. If that's your view, then I've failed miserably in writing this script.

> *I could dedicate multiple pages talking about the many success stories we've encountered in recent days.*

I certainly believe in living a prosperous life. I believe it is God's plan to bless us with more than enough. However, that is not the only mark of success and it is most definitely not the focus of reaching the other side. *The other side* is not about money. It's about living in a place of peace and happiness; knowing you refused to give up when the enemy attempted to destroy you.

It wasn't just our finances that the enemy attacked. He attacked every part of our lives. Although we faced financial ruin only a short time ago, we've been blessed far beyond everything lost. In addition to a life now filled with peace and contentment, we also declare abundance, greater than we could waste in ten lifetimes. It sounds like a bold confession of faith. But we believe it will someday move beyond a proclamation of faith and become an acknowledgement of God's blessing on our family.

The world said it was impossible to survive this storm, much less to be able to launch multiple business endeavors without any money. I'm happy to say, God had a different plan for our lives.

He spoke life in the face of death, abundance in the season of lack and happiness in the depths of despair. He offered grace when the world wanted justice. He is the foremost reason we are alive today.

When the enemy attempted to starve us out, God gave us an opportunity to feed others. When the storm said, "I'll take everything you have," God said, "I'll give you something the storm can't take away!"

The other side is about more than just financial stability. It's also about living in peace and harmony. It's about unity in your marriage and tranquility in your home. It's about a full supply, both of things essential and things not. It's about understanding who you are and why you were put on this earth.

It's about embracing your destiny as an individual while navigating the difficult seas of life and overcoming adversity and peril. It's about laying claim to the promises Christ gave His life to provide.

The other side is about living in a place free of anger, bitterness and animosity. A life free from the bondage and condemnation of sin and human imperfection.

It's about living in God's presence on a daily basis and knowing that He's as close as the mention of His name. It's about knowing that regardless of the delusion or dilemma you face, He is there to assist you. It's knowing that *anywhere* you go, He will be there with you.

And yes, it sounds a bit like the Garden of Eden. The very place He created for us.

Tammye and I have found a grace of living, accompanied by an assurance beyond measure, that we are loved unconditionally. We possess a purity of heart that transcends anything we've ever known previously.

Beyond business and ministry opportunities, the greater blessings have come in watching our family grow. Austin married the love of his life, Kaitlyn, who stands with him in tireless efforts to encourage and assist others. Together they are navigating their own path, their own personal journey of overcoming all of life's challenges.

It is such a joy to watch them grow in marriage and life, experiencing many blessings along the way. They too are committed to sharing the Good News with as many as possible whether through business, music, ministry or simply a hug and a smile. They truly are two of the most amazing people God ever put on the face of this planet.

Continuing the legacy of world changers, Austin and Kaitlyn's first baby, Graham Thomas Howell, made his appearance in June of 2015. The way he smiles and laughs is more than enough to make any day feel better. Like his father, he too loves to make music.

I can only imagine what God has in store for that little guy. Oh, how I love it when he takes me by the hand and leads me to the piano, just so we can sing together.

When Hollyn June Howell joined Graham's parade in August of 2017, the Garden once again asserted itself in grace and beauty. I never knew these beautiful angels were on *the other side* of our peril.

There's something special about being with Graham and Holly that makes *the other side* so much more than we ever dreamed. Tammye and I have often commented, "How blessed we are to be able to experience the joys of our family, together."

Satan tried vehemently to destroy us, but once again God wins!

We don't need fancy cars, fine clothes nor the best food. Just watching our family get together and laugh is worth more than the wealth of the world.

In 2016, Austin, Kaitlyn and Graham helped lead a very large team of volunteers on a trip to Mexico with Project Dream Seeds. Only a short time before, they served as youth pastors in a thriving new church. They left that work to serve on the mission field, recognizing that personal happiness often comes through serving the needs of others. Today, they serve humbly in many areas at The Bridge; as well as, assisting several other churches in the surrounding communities.

> *All that the enemy meant for harm, God turned into something very special.*

I can only tell you how proud I am of our family never giving up, never giving in. All that the enemy meant for harm, God turned into something very special.

Though our life is flourishing in many areas, we've vowed not to get lost in the hubris that melted our wings on more than one occasion.

We understand we will most likely face future dilemmas, possibly even storms of catastrophic proportion. To that end, we readily recognize our help comes from God. He is the center of our world, the true north of our compass.

It is beyond our ability in words to express our deepest gratitude for those who stood by us when things were the darkest. Those who loved us when we were unloveable and prayed over us when we couldn't pray over ourselves.

It is our pledge to offer the same support to others in our path, especially to those who may find themselves in similar distress. It is our commitment to be true *difference makers* for those we encounter. Each morning, our prayer is that we are able to assist someone and help them find the peace that fervently alluded us for so long.

It is our heartfelt prayer that the intimate details of our story will offer a sense of hope to others who struggle as we did.

Perhaps you will be able to identify your own adversities while reading our story. It's important to understand, regardless of the indiscretion or failure, whether on your part or someone else's, the Holy Spirit is reaching out to help you find restoration and reconciliation.

The details of your storm may look different on the surface, but deep down you will most likely identify with some of the same elements shared in this book. Regardless of whether or not the storm was in your marriage, your business, your health, finances or some other area, the same principles of promise apply.

You too can live in a place of peace and purpose, a place of hope and healing. Even though *the other side* may look somewhat different for you, it can still represent a fresh start and a haven of hope.

The most important element to retain from our story is that YOU can face the storms of life and survive. YOU can rise from the ashes. YOU can become a healthy and strong individual capable of facing any circumstance.

Allow God to give you a life of peace and happiness regardless of who else may or may not live that life with you. Allow yourself to move forward embracing a new season.

Though you will most likely never forget the horrors of your trials, allow yourself to live in the forgiveness and peace of knowing that no one and nothing will ever have the power to stop you from living the life of destiny God has called you to.

> *Today is a great day to start that journey.*

Today is a great day to start that journey.

Reach out to someone you trust and ask for help. Call the counselor and schedule an appointment. Check yourself into a rehabilitation facility. Join a support group. Read the book you've been ignoring.

Accept that invitation to church this Sunday. Make an honest altar and ask God to give you the strength and courage to face your fears and speak to your storm. Set a course for a place most only dream of.

Never before have Tammye and I enjoyed life so genuinely. We've discovered a joy not found in man's idea of success, not found on Wall Street nor in Beverly Hills. We've experienced a true miracle of restoration, both as individuals and as a family unit.

Recently, we traveled back to visit our friends in Ohio where we first heard those all-important words, *the other side*. But this time it was different. Our conversations were lively and joyous. The laughter was real. The smiles genuine.

People who knew us before often comment on how much we've changed and how different we are. Even Austin routinely offers his approval of the new Dave and Tammye. I can't begin to tell you how humbling this is. It is beyond fulfilling.

I don't ever want to go back to that ugly and lonely place of defeat. I don't ever again want to live in that despair. Not only do I hope to avoid it, I sincerely pray that these pages will offer some sense of direction allowing you to avoid it as well.

Every day Tammye and I are deeply grateful for our new life. It is such a great place to call home. It's a place we have dreamed of for many years. A place that captivated our thoughts, comforted our sleep and compelled us to forge ahead.

It's unlike any place we've ever known. It feels like we're living in a garden.

Chapter 30

Not the Final Chapter

Every book, play and movie have a final chapter. Sentences end with a period or another punctuation noting finality of the statement. Every game has a final segment. Every race a final lap.

Inherently, we like to close out portions of the process, giving a sense of completion. Even in life, we often view death as final, though it isn't. The flesh may give up its breath, but it is far from the end of our journey. In fact, it is typically referred to as "a time of transition" noting our indulgent belief in the afterlife.

We insist on embracing a mind-set of finality.

Even when it is blatantly obvious that we have reached anything but the end, we remain determined to place a period where a comma is needed. Something deep inside cries out for closure. We need to believe it's over, once and for all.

Even when it is blatantly obvious that we have reached anything but the end, we remain determined to place a period where a comma is needed.

But what if it isn't? What if there's more? What if there's another chapter to follow? What if there is another dark night, another storm or another challenging season? What if there's another problem, like the one you just came through?

Too often I hear people relate to the difficult season they've endured, saying, "I'll never go through that again. I'll never deal with that problem after today. I'm glad I'm finally through with that chapter of my life."

This would be great, especially if it were true. Unfortunately, it isn't. We do find ourselves dealing with more problems, more turmoil and more challenges. It's part of life and part of the process through which we continue to grow.

I would like to tell you there will never be another bad day or another problem. The truth is, until we get to heaven, we will continue to face opposition.

Most certainly, we need to find some degree of closure to our crisis. An internal means of accepting what has happened. Possibly even an acceptance, partial or whole, of responsibility for the chaos. In the very least, an acknowledgement of the dilemma.

This can provide a means whereby we position ourselves for the next season; but please understand, there will always be a sensitive place in our heart for the delicate seasons of our life.

Regardless of how we find our moment of closure, remember, it is only a moment. Tomorrow will still knock on our door and present another crisis.

Making it to *the other side* was a monumental accomplishment for Tammye and I. It was a journey of epic proportions. Most thought we would never make it. We even questioned its validity on more than one occasion.

Now that we've made it, what's the next step? Where do we go from here?

A dear friend who owns a marketing company shares a great story about a shampoo company trying to increase their sales. They decided to add a few simple words to the instructions on the shampoo bottle, "rinse and repeat."

By following the directions, "rinse and repeat," customers used more shampoo, thus allowing the company to increase its sales exponentially.

> ✺
> *Now that we've made it, what's the next step? Where do we go from here?*

If this sounds simple, then yes, it is. It is also akin to the principles necessary in finding success, again and again. Once we know what to do, we simply repeat that process whenever we face a similar problem.

In our journey to *the other side*, we learned valuable skills that have enabled us to find a certain degree of success. It would be foolish to abandon those skills. Instead, we are careful to remember them and apply the same fruitful principles again and again and again.

Without question, we've had days when an old problem wanted to rear its ugly head. There have been nights when sleep decided to abandon its purpose. Days when old emotions tried to rise from the ashes. Memories of darkness, yearning for the light of day. There were even a few brief seasons of challenges, reluctant to subside.

There were times when a familiar face, one we'd long pledged to forget, suddenly made a surprise appearance. The infamous name in a friend's social media thread or an accidental encounter at the market that tried to catch us unaware.

Suddenly, fear and depression became the uninvited visitors to our garden of peace and purpose.

It felt a bit like crashing my new car only minutes after leaving the dealership. In a moment, without warning or notice, the otherwise sunny day suddenly became dark and cloudy with a chance of storms.

It was crucial in those moments to take authority over the situation and dictate the rules and boundaries. We immediately recognized the need to take control of our emotions and refuse them permission to infect our harvest with vile delusions.

I can tell you with great certainty, we recognize the likelihood that those once formidable enemies still lurk in the shadows. With that in mind, Tammye and I have intently prepared ourselves for the moment.

We've made incredible strides. We've overcome the greatest obstacles of our life, and we've finally realized what true peace actually feels like.

We are determined that nothing and no one will ever be allowed to keep us from the life God has promised, the life we worked so hard to find.

"My doctors told me I would never walk again. My mother told me I would. I believed my mother."

The well-documented story of Wilma Rudolph accounts her premature birth on June 23, 1940, in St. Bethlehem, Tennessee, the 20th of 22 children. She went on to become a pioneering African-American track and field champion, but the road to victory was anything but easy.

Stricken with double pneumonia, scarlet fever and polio as a child, she had problems with her left leg and had to wear a brace. Though the doctors told her she would never walk, it was with great determination that she was able to overcome these challenges and rise to the level of a champion runner.

Nicknamed *"Skeeter"* for her famous speed, she qualified for the 1956 Summer Olympics in Melbourne, Australia. The youngest member of the U.S. track and field team at age sixteen she won a bronze medal in the 400 meter relay at those Olympic games.

In 1960, Rudolph returned to the world's greatest competition held in Rome, Italy, where she became the first American woman to win three gold medals in track and field at a single Olympic game.

She is remembered as one of the fastest women in track and as a source of great inspiration for generations of athletes.

She once stated, "Winning is great, sure, but if you are really going to do something in life, the secret is learning how to lose. Nobody goes undefeated all the time. If you can pick up after a crushing defeat and go on to win again, you are going to be a champion someday."[49]

Wilma Rudolph understood what it meant to face opposition. She also understood the meaning of determination. She refused to allow anything to hold her back from realizing her dreams. She truly embraced the heart of a champion.

Story after story of inspiring people throughout history offer a glimpse of the difficulties they faced. One thread of truth runs consistent through every one of their stories. Regardless of how many times you get knocked down, get back up.

We recognize this is not the final chapter. This is not the end. It is only part of the journey. There will always be another struggle, another challenge, another storm.

We are determined that we will not be defeated, and we will never give up. We will not allow temporary setbacks to keep us from our destiny. Failure is never final, and it will never be the last chapter in our story.

> ❧
> *Regardless of how many times you get knocked down, get back up.*

Accomplishing our goals and realizing our dreams will continually present opportunities for both success and failure. What we do with those opportunities will determine the etchings on our stone.

We boldly declare we are a winners! Overcomers! Victors, not victims!

We took the worst situations and made something good from them. We navigated the most horrific storms of life; and yet, we found the courage and strength to continue.

We refused to surrender to the colossal and vicious attacks from a heinous foe. We chose rather to speak peace over our tempest. Light over our darkness. Purpose over our problem and destiny over our disaster. Regardless of how the world sees us, when we look in the mirror, we see determined warriors.

Tammye and I still face challenges. Each day may bring a new set of circumstances. They may have fresh faces, but they are undeniably the same stale dilemmas.

We proudly and openly declare we are champions. We are winners. Regardless of what anyone else thinks about us, in our hearts we are victors.

More than anyone, we know the extremes of our rise, our fall and ultimately our rise again. Many of the intimate details of our struggles will hopefully never be known. We intentionally did not publish every minute account on these pages. Only God and that little bottle at sea truly know our darkest secrets. Then again, who else needs to know?

This is not our final chapter; but to this point, it is certainly one of our best.

There is something soothing about Tammye and I holding hands as we stroll through the park. Something appealing about our casual Sunday drive. Something fulfilling about sitting at the dinner table, enjoying a home cooked meal together.

I will forever remember the loneliness and emptiness of our home during that dark season. The cold embrace of an empty pillow. The lost purpose of a dining table. The restless nights yearning for companionship.

> *This is not our final chapter; but to this point, it is certainly one of our best.*

Thus, the reward of our relentless search for something special is appreciated all the more when our family gathers. The laughter seems louder. The stories are lighter. Even the good-byes are a gift, just knowing they are only temporary.

No longer do we hold our heads in shame as we walk through the market. No longer embarrassed for friends to ask how we're doing.

We've walked away from those infamous days of bitterness; as well as, the endless frustration that haunted our every thought. We found the hope, help and happiness that had managed to elude us for so many years.

You can also find the same peace and joy that we found. You can build the life you've been dreaming of. With God's help, persistence and the right tools, you can accomplish anything you set your heart to.

The conclusion of these pages finds us sharing more "vacations with purpose."

One such trip was Christmas in New York City. Though the city was magical in so many ways, the glisten of the lights nor the snowfall in Central Park compared to the peace in our hearts.

From a New Year's celebration at Niagara Falls with the family, to a private sunset cruise on a sailboat with friends, our life continues to unfold with peaceful days of bliss. All seeming to yield a similar tone: peace after the storm.

Today, we are truly living on *the other side*. It is without question the life we've dreamed of. More than that, we're living it together. It isn't just an abundance of physical pleasures; more so, it's the abundant peace that carries us through each day.

During the dark days, we read of a beautiful beach called Grace (Grace Bay Beach). It's one of the tranquil beaches of the Turks and Caicos Islands, peacefully planted in the beautiful Caribbean. We humbly asked God to let us someday visit that beach and joyously declare His "grace" over our lives.

Once again, God faithfully answered our prayers. With great peace and heartfelt emotions, Tammye and I shared the sunrise as we celebrated our 30th wedding anniversary on Grace beach. We walked that beautiful beach, hand in hand, in a tearful acknowledgement of God's overwhelming grace.

Recently, God blessed us with a beautiful new home—our dream home. That story would surely require many more chapters to tell how God brought it to pass in a miraculous fashion.

It's been comforting as many of our guests and friends have commented how they feel such *peace* in our new home. This too is a memorial of all that God has done.

It was an emotional time as friends gathered to help us dedicate and pray over our new home. Undeniably, it was one of the most humbling moments Tammye and I have ever experienced. You see, the day we dedicated our new dream home was exactly ten years to the day Tammye moved out.

As our journey continues, so too does our quest to find passion and purpose with each passing day. This is far from our final chapter. This is just the beginning of a whole new season, a season full of His peace and blessings.

Listen to me closely. With God by your side, you can overcome any storm. Regardless of how dark the clouds may be on your horizon, you can make it to *the other side*.

Ephesians 3:20-21 has overwhelmingly become an integral part of our daily conversations. I believe the Amplified translation offers unique clarity:

> *Now to Him who is able to [carry out His purpose and] do super-abundantly more than all that we dare ask or think [infinitely beyond our greatest prayers, hopes, or dreams], according to His power that is at work within us, **to Him be the glory**. . . .* [50]

Our family will forever be grateful for the endless grace and unconditional love Christ has shown to us. It is our greatest desire to help others find the same peace that we have found. The same forgiveness.

The same hope. And yes, the same dream of living where life is best, *The Other Side*.

Still Dreaming . . .
Dave & Tammye

THE CHALLENGE

It is my belief that you probably know someone else who needs the transforming and restorative revelations held within the pages of this book. The individual may be a pastor, business owner, co-worker, friend or companion. Regardless of their title, they are an acquaintance God has strategically put in your path.

Much like you and I once were, they are currently in a difficult place. Their marriage may be on the rocks. Their business or ministry may be teetering on the brink of disaster. They may feel all alone in their distress. More importantly, they may utterly be at the end their proverbial rope.

If you're like me, then you remember all too well how it feels to be in that lonely place.

I challenge you to sow into their life by giving them a copy of this book, along with your personal commitment to stand with them in support and friendship.

Write their name inside the cover of this book with a short pledge to support them. Remind them of their importance and value. Sign your name and give them your contact info.

Let them know you are available to help. You are not their counselor, their doctor, nor their therapist. You are their friend and accountability partner.

Pledge to check on them regularly and pray for them daily. Encourage them not to give up and always believe in the impossible.

Remind them, God is no respecter of persons. He loves them unconditionally and is ever present to hear their cry for help.

I pray you accept this challenge. If you do, I believe we will see many lives transformed.

Thanks for your pledge.
Dave Howell

A Note About Seeking Therapy

During the darkest days of our dilemma, we sought help not only from trusted friends and mentors, but also via professional counseling. Jim Grinnell, the senior therapist at Crossroads Counseling and Consultation was instrumental in helping us reach the other side with his sage wisdom along with both practical and godly insights. We would be remiss if we did not include the note below from him on the importance of this step on the road to recovery:

"Seeking out clinical therapy is an act of courage and an act of wisdom . . . though at first thought it sure doesn't seem like it. After all, who wants to let some flawed human stranger root around in the most sensitive areas of one's life, and when the hour is over, give that flawed person a wad of our hard-earned cash for the privilege? And yet the Scriptures say, *'He who conceals his transgressions* [brokenness] *will not prosper, but he who confesses and forsakes them will find compassion'"* (Proverbs 28:13 NASB).

"The truth is, we are all broken in one way or another. So often we need to break out of our own thoughts and compare our thoughts to the thoughts of how someone else might see our dilemma. We need someone else to listen to us without judgment, or hidden bias and someone who is not going to be overly protective of us if something hard needs to be said. We need someone to ask us artful questions that draw us into new ways of thinking about our distress. We also need to talk to someone who knows more than we do about the subject, so we can be educated in areas where we might be needlessly suffering because of a lack of knowledge. Who can do this important job for us?"

"A trained and skillful therapist is just such a person. If you are a person of faith, you want that therapist to be not only supportive of your faith, but also a practitioner who is well versed in the Scriptures and able to offer you 'best practice' clinical interventions and assignments that are congruent with biblically based values and strategies that will help you mature in your faith as well."

"A skillful therapist is formally trained in asking powerful questions, listening deeply, sensing clues to ways forward, saying hard but necessary things, detecting and exposing core beliefs that are working against your best interests, encouraging you in what you are doing well, and in most instances, educated in best practice research on the problem at hand. In almost every other part of life, when getting it right is critical, we want someone who is formally trained in what we need: whether it's installing a new furnace in our home, replacing a knee or doing brain surgery."

"In *The Other Side,* Pastor David rightly asks why we would subject our most intimate fears and thoughts and concerns—as well as our most sacred relationships to someone who is not formally trained in the human behavior and has not shown the dedication and perseverance necessary to get that training. So often, people reach out to friends and family for counsel, not realizing that it is next to impossible for those close to them to be impartial. This is one of the great lessons of the book of Job in the Bible, that friends and family tend not to be good counselors!"

"When the chips are down . . . when it's all on the line . . . in addition to your most trusted spiritual mentors, reach out to a clinically trained, biblically based counselor as well. Remember, the Scriptures admonish us that '*in a multitude of counsellors there is safety* [wisdom]' (Proverbs 11:14 KJV). When the stakes are high, you want to make sure you are getting competent, as well as compassionate advice and care."

—Jim Grinnell, Senior Therapist
Crossroads Counseling and Consultation
Tulsa, Oklahoma

Appendix A

A Magic Wind

This is the story of a young man, full of desire to be something good and great, to do things that would make a mark on mankind. Things that impact the lives of many.

I saw him, so young and eager, as he began his walk down the long road that's called life. He knew he would need something to sustain him in all situations. As he walked, he searched for that thing that would be his strength when the world turned on him. Suddenly, there by the roadside was a large bag, beautifully adorned with jewels and precious stones of all kinds.

The young man quickly opened it, and inside he found great knowledge and wisdom, and the answers to almost every possible question. He found solutions to problems that most young men stumbled over. Yes, this was surely what would make him a success. He picked up the bag and resumed his travel, confident that this was what he was searching for.

But, alas, as time went on, he began to use up all the answers that were in the beautiful bag. And the wisdom that he had counted on no longer seemed to be sufficient. He tried everything in the bag, but it was a losing battle and he began to weaken and fall under the bag's weight. Wearily, he left it all by the side of the road and struggled on.

Now, I see the man, no longer so young, searching the road for direction. But, what's this? He almost stumbles over a large box in the road. He opens the top of the old box and looks in, and found what just might be the answer he needs. The box contained dozens and dozens of friends. Young and old and all ages in between. The friends began hugging him and showering him with their love. They lifted him up and encouraged him and cared for him, and he was confident that this would be his key to the success he prayed for.

Now it's the middle of the day, and what has happened to all those who cared so much? One by one, as the journey continued, his friends began to disappear. Just when his success was dependent upon someone else, they seemed to vanish. He had emptied the old box of all its contents now, and once again he became weary, still trying to find the elusive success that he envisioned.

It now seemed that there was no hope of his vision ever becoming anything more than just a vision. And then out of nowhere, he suddenly felt a tiny breeze across his face. He reached out his hand and gently took hold of the breeze and placed it in his pocket.

As he continued down the old road, he passed through a valley that was very low between the mountain peaks. The trail was hidden from the sunlight, and soon he began to feel a chill. It was then that he reached into his pocket and took out the magic wind. As he opened his hand, the wind became a warm and soothing cloak around him, and he felt strong and encouraged to go on.

Soon his journey took him into the desert. It was the middle of the afternoon, and the sun began to beat down on him. He was weary and started to fall in the midst of the blazing heat. Then he remembered the magic wind. He reached into his pocket and when he opened his hand, the magic wind became a cool breeze. The refreshing breeze continued to shield him from the heat of the desert until he was out of danger.

Finally, I see the fully matured man. It's evening now, and still he searches for fulfillment of his dreams. And now something lies ahead.

Enemies from all sides seem to surround him. This surely must be the end of the vision.

Weakened from his day long journey, maybe it's time to give up. With faltering hope, he reaches again into his pocket and removes one more handful of the magic wind. As he opens his hand, that same magic wind that earlier in the day had been a soothing warmth when he was cold, and then a gentle cooling breeze in the desert heat, suddenly becomes a fierce and terrible storm. All around him it whirls, the wind destroying everything in its path. His enemies, that were pressing in on him, now were swept away in one horrifying moment. All of this while he stood motionless in the peaceful eye of the storm.

And now the day is far spent. The road winds to an end, and I see the man as he reflects upon his journey and realizes that he has accomplished many of the things that were in his vision. He ponders on his success and realizes that it wasn't the jeweled bag with wisdom and knowledge, nor the old box with many friends that had brought him to this place.

No, it was undoubtedly the magic wind that he had captured and used when needs arose. Now, one final time he reaches into his pocket and takes out the last of the magic wind. He slowly opens his hand and the wind begins to swirl, gently at first, then progressively stronger. Soon it becomes a mighty whirlwind, filled with smoke and fire, and begins gently lifting the old man upward into a new place where he's never been before.

At last it becomes clear to him. He suddenly understands the magic of the wind. This wind that he held in his hand, that was always there when he needed it, that took care of him in every situation, was not magic at all.

It was simply the breath of Almighty God.

This story was written and given to me many years ago during a difficult season. I cherished it and vowed never to forget its truest meaning. Along the way, I placed it in a secure place to protect it and keep it from being lost or destroyed. Through the years, though I had never forgotten the story, I somehow lost track of where I had placed the written copy. Regretfully, I feared that I had lost it. For a great deal of time, I searched and prayed that I could recover this lost gem and once again glean from its strength. A few days ago, while doing a bit of cleaning, I discovered a small fireproof box that I had purchased more than twenty-five years ago. Within it were several documents and memorabilia. To my pleasure and surprise, it also contained the original writing of *"A Magic Wind."*

I could hardly contain myself. Tears flowed without resistance as I opened the envelope and began to read the story once again. Together, Tammye and I poured over the pages with a sense of comfort and peace.

This was no accidental find. This was without question an answer to prayer. Possibly, the angel of lost things had supernaturally revealed to me the location. Or just possibly, it was that magic wind once again showing the beauty and grace unveiled in the story.

The timing of this find was perfect, in that the manuscript of this book was about to be printed. Without question, this story had to be inserted.

What I failed to mention, was the author of this little sonnet. To him I give credit, not only for this amazing story of the magic wind, but also for a lifetime of encouragement and support.

You see, since the day I was born, someone has been watching over every move I've made, guiding me, correcting me and loving me, all without regard to my success or failure.

It was he who taught me to play guitar before I had even started to school. He taught me how to fish and hunt. How to ride a bicycle. How to build electronic gadgets from a blueprint. How to fly an airplane, and so much more.

More than anything, he taught me the value of God and family. He taught me to never forget to pray, never underestimate the power of God and never disregard the importance of covering my family. Most importantly, he taught me to never ever give up.

I remember one specific season; unfortunately, it was a difficult time for Tammye and I. We were considering our future, if we had one at all. It was during this time I was given a powerful tenant of truth. "Love is not always a feeling. Sometimes it is a decision."

On that day, and every day since, I've made a conscious decision to choose my family. To this day, I am grateful, not only for those words and this poem, but for a lifetime of love and support. You've been more than a biological father. You've also been my friend and a godly example of how a real man should live.

Thank you Pop Howell.

Appendix B

That Girl with the Hair
(I wrote this poem for Tammye on our 29th Anniversary)

T'was the week before Christmas, and all thru the town;
Every starlet was sparkling, only one would be found.
Her smile was electric, with eyes hazel green;
Her clothes were eclectic. She dressed like a queen.
T'was a wedding, then pizza; with snow in the air;
That skinny little preacher. That girl with the hair.

She gave him a tie. He gave her a kiss;
She opened her heart. Love couldn't resist.
She giggled. She wiggled. Oh how she could dance;
He couldn't. He shouldn't! Don't give him a chance.
They laughed and they lived. No dream could compare;
That funny little preacher. That girl with the hair.

To the right and the left, their path would embrace;
Soon to be challenged, their gifts and their faith.
Their light would be brighter. Their love would abide;
Beyond every storm; behold, the other side.
It's hard to imagine, or even compare;
Unshakable that preacher. That girl with the hair.

To the core, it is red; maybe strawberry too;
But never undone, there's always a do.
They're fashion. They're hip. They're always in step;
Still beaming. Still dreaming. There's more coming yet.
They cling to each other, and a hand in the air;
That silly ole preacher. That girl with the hair.

dch   3.3.17

ABOUT THE AUTHOR

Dave Howell is the co-founder of Premier USA, a staffing and consulting company; and The Bridge at Christ Church, a nondenominational church where he serves as Lead Pastor.

Dave also works with his son Austin in Howell Sound Company, selling pro audio, video and lighting gear; as well as, offering a full production music studio.

He is a graduate of Rhema Bible College and also attended Victory Bible College where he helped establish the School of Worship, facilitating several areas of study and serving as Assistant Director.

After a season in Oklahoma City, Dave returned to Muskogee, where he established several successful businesses and ministry objectives. He routinely serves on a handful of boards and committees in various communities. He is recognized for his keen insights and unique perspective.

His expansive musical gifts as singer, songwriter and artist have afforded many opportunities to connect with a wide array of audiences across the nation. He performs at a high level behind several instruments. He can usually be found behind a guitar or piano laying down an inspiring groove. Currently, he serves as Vice President of the Oklahoma Music Hall of Fame.

Dave is widely known as the "Faster Pastor" from his years in dirt track racing. He not only drove, but also found creative ways to share the Gospel on his way to Victory Lane. He was always careful to note that his racing career was more about changing lives than winning races. To his credit, he accomplished both with great success.

He frequently travels to Puerto Vallarta, Mexico, with Project Dream Seeds where he helps facilitate the needs of underserved children; as well as, mentoring and coaching local business leaders, teachers and pastors.

In the board room, on stage or behind the scenes Dave is equally comfortable with the various roles in which he is called to serve.

He is a true "Okie from Muskogee," who was born and raised in the hills of northeastern Oklahoma where he and Tammye still reside. They have one son, Austin, who serves alongside his father in many capacities. Without question, the best part of Dave's day is time spent with family, especially his grandchildren, Graham and Hollyn.

Dave is quick to note his life is most fulfilling with Tammye, the love of his life, by his side. Together, they truly believe they can change the world.

Endnotes

Chapter 1
1 Songwriters, Paul Williams & Roger Nichols. "We've Only Just Begun" lyrics, copyright © Universal Music Publishing Group, Tratore.

Chapter 2
2 John 5:30 NIV.
3 See Ephesians 5:16.

Chapter 4
4 Jack Collis. Michael LeBoeuf. Published 2007 by B Jain Books; published 1994 by Dabara Publisher.

Chapter 5
5 See Matthew 19:26.

Chapter 12
6 Luke 23:34 NIV
7 Psalm 23:4 NKJV.
8 See Matthew 5:45.

Chapter 14
9 Job 1:1 NIV.
10 See John 10:10.
11 2 Corinthians 12:10 NIV.
12 Romans 8:28 NIV.

Chapter 15
13 Luke 22:32 NIV.
14 Proverbs 24:16 NLT.
15 See John 21:15-17.

Chapter 18
16 1 Corinthians 12:31 AMP.
17 1 Corinthians 13:4-8,13 AMP.
18 1 Corinthians 14:1 AMP.

Chapter 22
19 Isaiah 40:29-31 KJV.
20 Isaiah 40:31 KJV.
21 2 Corinthians 5:7 KJV.
22 Galatians 5:16 KJV.

23 Galatians 5:25 KJV.
24 Genesis 3:8 KJV.
25 Genesis 5:24 KJV.
26 Isaiah 40:31 KJV.
27 Hebrews 12:1 KJV.
28 Philippians 2:16 KJV.
29 Philippians 2:16 AMP (2015).
30 Proverbs 25:15 NIV.
31 Isaiah 40:31 KJV.
32 James 1:2-4 NLT.
33 2 Corinthians 4:17-18 NIV.
34 Ecclesiastes 7:8 NLT.
35 Psalm 30 MSG. (abbreviated).

Chapter 23
36 Psalm 23:6 KJV.
37 Psalm 46:1 KJV.
38 James 1:13 NLT.
39 See 2 Timothy 1:5.
40 John 10:10 NIV.
41 Ephesians 6:11 KJV.
42 See 2 Corinthians 2:11 AMP. (2015).

Chapter 24
43 Matthew 19:26 KJV.

Chapter 25
44 Psalm 37:23-24 NLT.
45 See Mark 9:23.
46 James 2:20 NKJV.
47 James 1:21 KJV.

Chapter 27
48 Proverbs 27:17 NKJV.

Chapter 30
49 www.biography.com/athlete/wilma-rudolph.
50 Ephesians 3:20-21 AMP. (2015).